FARMERS' MARKET
DESSERTS

FARMERS' MARKET DESSERTS

GORGEOUS FRUIT RECIPES FROM FIRST-PRIZE PEACH PIE
TO EASY CHOCOLATE CHERRY CUPCAKES

BY JENNIE SCHACHT

PHOTOGRAPHS BY LEO GONG

CHRONICLE BOOKS
SAN FRANCISCO

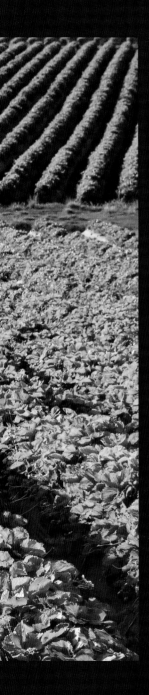

Library of Congress Cataloging-in-Publication Data available.

ISBN 978-0-8118-6672-9

Manufactured in China

Designed by **MICHAEL MORRIS**
Food and prop styling by **KIM KISSLING**

The photographer wishes to thank all of the farmers who shared their lives with us; friends and family who gave us a home as we traveled; Kim for her beautiful food and prop styling; and most important, my wife, Harumi, for all of her love, support, and companionship throughout this creative endeavor.

10 9 8 7 6 5 4 3 2 1

Chronicle Books LLC
680 Second Street
San Francisco, CA 94107
WWW.CHRONICLEBOOKS.COM

The people who give you their food give you their heart.

—CESAR CHAVEZ

With love and profound admiration, this book is dedicated to the farmers, market operators, and proponents of local eating and sustainable agriculture who make the bounty of the market available to us all.

Also to Birdi, who cannot be resisted when she beseeches, "Cherry pie?"

ACKNOWLEDGMENTS

A cookbook with a single name on the cover looks like a solo operation. In fact, it is always a team effort, and I would like to thank my MVPs here.

At Chronicle Books, I thank Bill LeBlond for believing in the idea; Sarah Billingsley for carrying through the details; Michael Morris for a beautiful design; Peter Perez and David Hawk for their enthusiastic marketing and publicity efforts; and Doug Ogan, Ben Kasman, and the many others who consistently produce books that are beautiful to look at and a pleasure to use. Sharon Silva is the kind of editorial wizard with whom a writer dreams about working: smart, clever, observant, and kind.

I am in awe of Leo Gong's gorgeous photography and also thank his wife and assistant, Harumi Shimizu. "Charming wife" sounds like a cliché, but in this case it's a perfect fit. Leo and Harumi went miles—literally—beyond the call of duty to capture markets in several regions. Kim Konecny Kissling used her artistic eye and unstoppable attention to detail to style the desserts for the camera, aided by her able and affable assistant, Sarah Fairhurst.

I owe a mountain of debt to my literary agent, Carole Bidnick, who does not stop with the sale of the concept to the publisher, but rather follows her authors' every step, always ready to lend an ear or a hand to keep things moving along smoothly.

There would be no book if not for the farms, farmers, and markets who make it all happen. I wish I could have visited and paid tribute to every one of them. Luckily, I live in beautiful Northern California with its Mediterranean climate, and have friends and family in Seattle, North Central Wisconsin, and New York's Hudson Valley, all bountiful with agricultural products and markets to share them. The Sources & Resources section will help you find markets in your area, as well as the farmers and producers mentioned in this book.

Many people pointed me in the direction of their favorite producers and markets, including David Hughes and Gabrielle Langholtz of New York's Greenmarket; Dan Barber of Stone Barns Center for Food & Agriculture; Leda Meredith, avid New York locavore and author of *Botany, Ballet & Dinner from Scratch: A Memoir with Recipes*; and Miriam Haas of Westchester County Community Markets. In Wisconsin, George and Sue Grimm led me to the incomparable Weston's Antique Apples, and all of the Burishes escorted me to markets and farms and introduced me to their farmer friends. In the San Francisco Bay Area, Peggy Knickerbocker, John Birdsall, and Lesley Stiles helped set my path.

The recipes work because a swarm of voluntary testers was kind enough to take them out for a test drive and offer their feedback. They include Angela Davies, Janis Burger, Marilyn Davison, Patty Burch, Philip Cooper, Elizabeth Statmore, Becky McIver, and Holly Krasner. Special thanks go to those testing the most recipes: Kathy Andre, Marjorie Goldfarb, Emily Lichtenstein, Linda Yoshino, and the generous and talented Sara Goepfrich. Rachel Boller gave Sara a run for her money, hopping on board near the end and testing a remarkable number of recipes in a short time with great enthusiasm and expert feedback.

Others offered valuable guidance, including Flo Braker, Mary Cech, Nancy Kux, Mickie Weinberg, and Lynne Devereux, who shared not only cheese advice but also her supply of Cypress Grove's wonderful goat's milk fromage blanc. Many members of the Bay Area Bakers Dozen kindly provided troubleshooting assistance.

CONTENTS

A VISIT TO THE MARKET

When I go to the farmers' market, I almost always have something sweet in mind. There is no better pie than one made with summertime's fragrant peaches, no better cobbler than one filled with juicy berries picked that morning at dawn, no better ice cream than one churned with brilliant orange tangerines.

No matter where you live, chances are you will find a farmers' market not far away. You might not associate Rhode Island with farming, but that small state has more than twenty-five markets, and Alaska has nearly twenty. In the San Francisco Bay Area, you can shop a different market every day of the week. In fact, there are farmers' markets—and farms—in every state.

According to the United States Department of Agriculture (USDA), in 2008, more than 4,600 farmers' markets were operating throughout the United States, an increase of about 1,000 markets, or about 26 percent, over the 2004 figure. Since the USDA began publishing its National Directory of Farmers Markets in 1994, markets have grown 167 percent, with nearly 3,000 new markets springing up.

If you explore the markets within your reach—and especially if you become a regular shopper at the one you like best—things start to happen: you feel more connected to the seasons; you can't wait to find out what your favorite grower has to offer; you look forward to each trip because you feel

so good when you're there; you make new friends; and you finally understand why the bland imported supermarket plums you were purchasing out of season taste nothing like the bursting-with-juice real thing.

Why Shop at a Farmers' Market?

Unless you have a backyard garden or visit farms directly, a farmers' market is your best bet for finding locally grown food at its freshest. In fact, although there is great satisfaction in growing your own fruits and vegetables, purchasing them at the market assures they were grown under optimal conditions by people who know how to coax the best from their plants and trees, typically with potentially harmful chemicals kept to a minimum or completely out of the picture.

The health value of consuming locally grown produce is so well established that Kaiser Permanente, one of the nation's leading managed-care organizations, began operating a weekly farmers' market at its Oakland, California, medical center in 2003, a move spearheaded by Dr. Preston Maring, a Kaiser obstetrician-gynecologist. Thanks to his steadfast dedication, today Kaiser operates thirty markets in Northern and Southern California, Oregon, Georgia, and Hawaii. Dr. Maring prescribes recipes to his patients on his blog, and if you are lucky enough to sit down with him at the Oakland market, he can tell you something about nearly every vendor and customer there, including the evolving dietary habits of the two intervention radiologists on their lunch hour who stroll by.

Shopping the market also ensures that fresh, locally grown produce will be available when you need it. Much of the fruit in your local supermarket is invariably centrally sourced, picked unripe to allow for travel, and comes from thousands of miles away, but farmers' market produce is local and picked at its peak. It's the best of one-stop shopping,

The family-run Glaum Egg Ranch brings fresh-tasting eggs to the market from its 28-acre spread in the foothills of Santa Cruz County, California, where chickens roam free and dine on an organic vegetarian diet. The ranch is a USDA and California Certified Organic Farm and a member of the Community Alliance with Family Farmers (CAFF), a group dedicated to supporting family farms.

with many of the fresh foods you need for the week under one big umbrella. And in the case of seasonal desserts, you will find not only the fruits you need, but also often the eggs, butter, yogurt, maple syrup, honey, and other ingredients that go into these luscious treats.

When you purchase your produce at the farmers' market, the price you pay goes directly to the farmers and their local operations. Your supermarket dollar goes to transportation, packaging, advertising, and a host of other costs that have little to do with the fruit you are buying. Although the price you pay at your local farmers' market is sometimes higher—family farms are expensive to run—you know that every dollar stays in your community, and that benefits you.

Vendors bring produce varieties to the market that would be too fragile to ship. These are often the most flavorful types and are rarely, if ever, seen in a grocery store. Most times, the produce will last longer because it is sold to you fresher. And if you aren't satisfied, you can talk directly to the vendor the next time you visit the market. (Don't forget to let vendors know how happy you are when things go well, too!)

Farmers' markets are an important income source for many of the farmers who sell at them. Indeed, without market patronage, some would be unable to maintain their farm businesses. In 2000, nineteen thousand farmers around the country reported to the USDA that they were selling their produce at farmers' markets only. The family that operates Wilklow Orchard in Highland, New York, credits the markets with saving the farm by providing the lion's share of their profits, allowing them to grow.

While writing this book, I have become friends with farmers and other market vendors who once felt like strangers. I am a little shy, and although I always knew I could benefit from knowing the people who grow the food I eat, striking up a conversation had been hard. This book

Yukio Hamada of Hamada Farms says that although only about 20 percent of his produce goes to farmers' markets, those sales contribute more than half of his annual profit because there is no middleman. Hamada, along with his three adult children and fifteen full-time and thirty-five seasonal workers, grows persimmons, apples, apricots, avocados, Asian pears, cherries, cucumbers, eggplants, figs, lemons, melons, nectarines, nuts, quinces, peaches, plums, Pluots, grapes, walnuts, and exotic citruses, such as Oroblancos, Cocktail grapefruits, and Tahitian pomelos on his 235-acre farm in Kingsburg, California. If you roam the orchards when the workers are tending plants and harvesting fruits, you will see they enjoy their work.

gave me a reason to talk to the vendors, and I quickly realized that I didn't need a reason. Vendors are just as hungry to connect with their customers as we are to connect with them. They will be delighted to hear what you did with the sour cherries you bought the week before or what you will do with the boysenberries you are buying that day. They are full of stories about the joys and frustrations of their work.

Farmers' Market Desserts

There is no denying that much of the produce found at farmers' markets is thoroughly enjoyable eaten out of hand. But when it's time to welcome guests, woo a heartthrob, celebrate a special occasion, thank a friend, let your family know you love them, or simply satisfy a craving, nothing is better than a dessert made at home with the finest ingredients. My favorite desserts are made with fresh fruits (and occasionally vegetables), dried fruits, nuts, and sweet sticky honey and maple syrup. So before I head into the kitchen, I start with a trip to the farmers' market.

Most of the time, I don't know what I'm going to make until I see what is laid out on the tables and piled high in the bins. I wander the market, sampling the wares and chatting with vendors or other shoppers. Then I head home with my loot and think about the desserts I might prepare. Will I bake a pie with the ripe, rosy-skinned peaches, or should I roast them and top them with ice cream and raspberry sauce? If the strawberries are ripe and juicy, I might fold them into whipped cream and wrap them in a cake roll. Or, if I'm thinking ahead to tomorrow's breakfast, I might bake them into a buckwheat-flecked tea cake that does double duty: a lovely dessert tonight and a welcome sight on the morning table. In the fall, I'm ready to choose apples to fill with caramel and wrap in pastry, and I know I can beat the winter doldrums if I'm fortified with vivid orange tangerine ice cream.

This book reflects my market visits over the course of a year, in which I took stock of what was available and then allowed the character of what I bought to shine in my favorite types of dessert. It moves through each season's star ingredients and ends with chapters highlighting market surprises available only regionally or not typically associated with desserts; sticky market sweeteners that can be used to embellish other market buys or as flavorings in their own right; and finally, dried fruits, nuts, and herbs that will have you enthusiastically turning out something sweet even when the market tables are nearly barren.

Many of the recipes include a Farm Journal note that relates a particular farm's or market's perspective on a given ingredient, or shares information on ingredients or techniques gleaned from markets and farms. Season to Taste notes encourage you to adjust the recipes to fit what is available at your own farmers' market, adapting them to other seasons and to the local harvest.

What's in Season?

Produce seasons vary regionally, but the table opposite provides a general guide to the peak U.S. growing season for much of the produce used in the recipes. Location may shift the season a month or two in either direction, and in areas with long growing seasons, many of these items are available for several months on either side of their peak season.

PRODUCE	JAN	FEB	MAR	APR	MAY	JUN	JUL	AUG	SEP	OCT	NOV	DEC
Almond								■	■	■		
Apple								■	■	■	■	
Apricot					■	■	■					
Avocado								■	■	■	■	■
Beet	■	■			■	■		■	■	■	■	■
Blackberry					■	■	■	■	■			
Blueberry					■	■	■	■				
Boysenberry					■	■	■					
Carrot	■	■	■	■	■	■	■	■	■	■	■	■
Cherry					■	■	■	■				
Corn						■	■	■	■			
Cranberry									■	■	■	■
Cucumber						■	■	■	■			
Date								■	■	■	■	■
Fig						■	■	■	■	■		
Grape							■	■	■	■	■	
Grapefruit	■	■	■	■	■						■	■
Hazelnut	■	■							■	■	■	■
Honey	■	■	■								■	■
Kumquat	■	■	■								■	■
Lemon	■	■	■	■	■	■	■	■	■	■	■	■
Lime	■	■	■	■	■	■	■	■	■	■	■	■
Mandarin	■	■	■								■	■
Maple syrup		■	■	■								
Melon						■	■	■	■			
Nectarine					■	■	■	■	■			
Orange	■	■	■	■	■						■	■
Peach					■	■	■	■	■			
Pear	■							■	■	■	■	■
Persimmon										■	■	■
Pineapple				■	■	■	■	■				
Plum					■	■	■	■	■			
Pomegranate	■								■	■	■	■
Pumpkin									■	■	■	
Quince									■	■	■	
Raspberry					■	■	■	■	■	■		
Rhubarb				■	■	■	■					
Strawberry			■	■	■	■	■					
Walnut	■	■	■						■	■	■	■
Winter squash									■	■	■	■
Tangerine	■	■									■	■
Zucchini					■	■	■	■	■			

■ IN SEASON

With the market's most enticing produce packed carefully into your basket, it's time to head back to the kitchen. What follows are some of my favorite tools, ingredients, techniques, and tips for making great desserts, along with two master recipes used throughout the book.

Equipment

In addition to the usual bowls, measuring cups and spoons, knives (sharp, please!), and the like, the following tools will help you to spend your time in the kitchen productively, yield reliable results, and—most important—have fun. The Sources & Resources section beginning on page 200 includes several good suppliers.

BAKING MATS AND PARCHMENT PAPER | Instead of using non-stick baking sheets, which can yield uneven results, invest in a couple of silicone baking mats. The mats can be used over and over, and they do a great job of preventing most baked items from sticking, making cleanup easier. If you don't have a silicone baking mat, line your baking sheets and cake pans with parchment paper according to recipe instructions. Parchment can be purchased in sheets and rounds to fit square, rectangular, and round cake pans, or purchased in a roll and cut to size.

BAKING SHEETS | Use heavy-gauge aluminum baking sheets to avoid buckling. A rimmed baking sheet will prevent ingredients from dripping over the side or rolling out of the pan. The half-sheet size (about 17 by 12 inches) is ideal for the recipes in this book. For some recipes, flat baking sheets are preferred, either because they offer better heat circulation or because they ease transfer from the baking sheet to another surface. Some baked goods brown more quickly on baking sheets with a dark finish, so keep an eye on what is in the oven and reduce the oven temperature, if needed, to prevent overbrowning.

BENCH SCRAPER | This handy tool—a straight-edged, broad stainless-steel blade outfitted with a wood, rolled metal, or molded plastic handle—is useful for keeping pastry mobile as you roll it; gathering and transporting small quantities of chopped nuts, citrus zest, or other ingredients; portioning dough; and scraping flour or sticky bits of dough from a cutting or rolling surface.

CAKE PANS | Look for shiny, heavy, light-colored aluminum or aluminized-steel pans with 2-inch sides. Dark pans can yield cakes with a tough, overbrowned crust. Glass pans conduct and hold heat well, risking overbaking. If you must use them, reduce the oven temperature by 25 degrees. Spring-form pans should have 3-inch sides and a tight seal between the outer ring and the base.

CHERRY PITTER | Available at many hardware and cookware stores, a handheld cherry pitter turns a difficult chore into a manageable one. Look for a pitter with a splash guard to help contain the juices, though an apron is also in order. I found my favorite pitter at C. J. Olson Cherries in Sunnyvale, California (see Sources & Resources). Developed by tool and die maker Otto Krasberg, the ingenious Push Button Cherry Pitter consists of a canning jar lid with a rubber strip clipped underneath and a spring-loaded plunger on top. You simply screw the top onto an ordinary canning jar, place a cherry over the hole, press the plunger, and the pit falls into the jar for easy collection.

CITRUS SQUEEZERS | Originally used primarily by bartenders, handheld citrus juicers are now widely sold color-coded for lemons, limes, and oranges. I find the middle (lemon) size works for all but the largest citrus fruits, which can be cut into pieces or juiced with a reamer or fork.

DOUBLE BOILER | A double boiler—a set of two pans, one resting snugly on top of the other—allows you to stir ingredients over more gentle heat than directly over the burner. You can purchase universal double-boiler inserts, but be sure you have a pan into which the insert will fit securely. You can create a makeshift double boiler by nesting a metal or other heat-resistant bowl securely over a saucepan to create a tight fit. When you use a double boiler—purchased or makeshift—always be sure the water in the bottom pan does not come in direct contact with the bottom of the top pan or bowl.

ELECTRIC MIXER | A standing mixer is the best tool for mixing ingredients that require more time than you wish to hold a handheld mixer. The paddle attachment is perfect for creaming, and the whisk attachment easily creates mounds of fluffy egg whites or cream. If you don't own a standing mixer, a good handheld electric mixer can handle most tasks.

GRATERS AND ZESTERS | Modeled after a woodworker's rasp, Microplane graters and zesters in many sizes make easy work of zesting citrus fruits, removing only the flavorful colored portion and avoiding the bitter pith beneath. They are also useful for grating nutmeg or chocolate.

ICE-CREAM MAKER | An inexpensive electric ice-cream maker is handy for making smooth sorbets and ice creams. If using the type that has a freezer bowl, be sure to freeze the bowl for 24 hours or longer before operating, and have the ice-cream mixture well chilled.

IMMERSION BLENDER | This may be my single favorite kitchen tool because it saves me from having to drag out the blender or food processor. It can be used to blend a mixture right in the saucepan, and when paired with its accessory chopper bowl, it simplifies cutting up small quantities of fruits, nuts, herbs, ginger, or other ingredients.

KITCHEN SCALE | For the most reliable results, bakers typically weigh their ingredients, rather than use volume measures. In general, the only ingredients in this book that are called for by weight, other than whole fruits and the like, are packaged ingredients that include the weight on the wrapper. However, if you purchase a large block of chocolate, a scale is the only way to know if you have cut off the quantity for a particular recipe. I prefer an electronic scale that displays both ounces and grams and has a removable platform for easy cleaning.

PIE AND TART PANS | Here, I depart from my usual preference for light-colored pans. The extra heat absorption guaranteed by a dark tart pan ensures a well-browned, crisp crust. Most are made of tin-plated steel and have a fluted edge that creates an attractive crust. A removable bottom makes it easy to unmold the finished tart: balance the pan over a small glass or bowl and the ring drops away, leaving the tart on the base for serving or for transferring to a serving platter with the aid of a wide metal spatula or small, rimless baking sheet. For pies, I prefer a clear glass dish so I can view the crust browning on the bottom. Ceramic pie pans can be attractive but make doneness more difficult to gauge.

PIZZA WHEEL | A sharp-bladed metal pizza wheel makes quick work of cutting a crostata or galette, scoring dough, and similar tasks.

RAMEKINS | Small ceramic baking dishes, available in a wide range of shapes, sizes, and colors, are useful for baking and serving a variety of desserts. If you are unsure of the capacity of a ramekin, fill it with water and then pour the water into a measuring cup. An 8-ounce ramekin holds 1 cup water, and a 6-ounce one holds ¾ cup. Ramekins and other ovenproof ceramic dishes are perfect for custards, pots de crème, and individual crisps.

ROLLING PIN | I prefer the lighter French-style long, tapered wooden pin, but the heavier traditional straight rolling pin with offset handles is also efficient for rolling out pie, tart, and other doughs. A silicone pad marked with dimensions simplifies measuring and peeling away the dough from the work surface. Once you get accustomed to it, rolling pastry between two sheets of lightly floured plastic film eases rolling and transferring the rolled-out dough to a pie or tart pan.

SAUCEPANS | Choose heavy saucepans made of nonreactive material such as anodized aluminum, stainless steel, or enamel-coated cast iron, in a variety of sizes. To avoid discoloration and off flavors from the interaction of the metal with acidic ingredients like citrus juices, stay away from nonanodized aluminum and use cast iron only when specified.

SCOOPS | These handy tools are for more than ice cream! Ice cream scoops in various sizes are helpful for uniformly scooping cookie dough, neatly transferring batter to individual pans such as muffin tins, and other kitchen tasks.

SPATULAS | Flat metal spatulas with a long, flexible blade come in many sizes. Offset spatulas, with a bend between the blade and the handle, are easier to control and are indispensable for smoothing batters, transferring cookies to cooling racks, frosting cakes, and other tasks. A large, wide spatula is helpful for moving delicate cakes, cake layers, and tarts. (A small rimless baking sheet also works well.) For scraping the sides of mixing bowls clean, folding ingredients, and stirring hot mixtures on the stove top, use flexible, heat-resistant silicone spatulas, available in a variety of sizes for tasks big and small.

WHISKS | A large balloon whisk is the best tool for incorporating air quickly and efficiently into egg whites and cream when you are not using an electric mixer. A flat whisk is perfect for stirring sauces, puddings, and similar hot mixtures in a saucepan, reaching easily into corners and smoothing out any lumps.

Ingredients

Most ingredients are described in the recipes. A few used frequently throughout the book warrant additional description.

BUTTER | Use the finest-quality butter you can find and afford for recipes in which butter is a major ingredient, such as pie crusts and butter cookies. Unless otherwise specified, use unsalted butter for the freshest flavor and best control of the amount of salt in the recipe. Softened butter should bend easily without breaking and should not be at all melted. For recipes calling for cold butter, leave it in the refrigerator until you are ready to use it. Some of my favorite butter brands are Land O'Lakes, Kerrygold, and Straus Family Creamery's European Style Butter.

CHOCOLATE AND COCOA POWDER | Many good brands of chocolate are available, including Callebaut, Divine (a fair trade product), El Rey, Guittard (and their E. Guittard line), Michel Cluizel, and Valrhona. Chocolate chips are made to hold their shape when baked, so they are best saved for cookies unless they are specified in a recipe. No strict definitions exist for bittersweet and semisweet chocolate, so in this book, in recipes that call for bittersweet chocolate, buy chocolate with a cacao content of 60 to 70 percent; and in those using semisweet chocolate, look for bars labeled 50 to 59 percent cacao.

Cocoa powder is chocolate with most of its cocoa butter removed, then ground to a powder. Dutch-processed (alkalized) cocoa powder makes desserts with an appealing dark chocolate color, but many bakers agree that natural (nonalkalized) cocoa powder has a deeper chocolate flavor. Among my favorite brands are Ghirardelli, Guittard, and Penzeys.

CREAM | For the most consistent results, especially in desserts that need to set, such as pots de crème or panna cotta, look for heavy cream that contains no additives or emulsifiers and is not ultrapasteurized.

FLOUR | Use the type of flour called for in the recipe, unless specific substitutions are suggested. Most of my recipes call for unbleached all-purpose flour. I store flour that won't be used right away in the freezer for the freshest flavor and to ensure cool dough for the flakiest pastry.

SALT | Most recipes in the book call for kosher salt. Look for a brand that carries no additives, which can impart chemical or other off flavors. Fine sea salt also has a clean taste and dissolves easily. If you have it on hand, substitute one-half the amount of kosher salt called for in the recipe. A few recipes specifically use sea salt or gray salt for its briny taste, fleur de sel for its delicate flavor, or Maldon sea salt for its flaky texture.

SUGAR | Pure cane sugar is more reliable than beet sugar. Superfine sugar (also labeled ultrafine, bar, castor, or caster sugar) dissolves more readily because its grains are smaller. My go-to sugar is C&H brand Baker's Sugar, with grains that fall between regular granulated and superfine sugar. It can be substituted for either sugar in equal quantity.

Confectioners' sugar, also known as powdered sugar, is finely ground granulated sugar mixed with a very small amount of cornstarch to keep it free-flowing. It creates a sandy texture in certain pie crusts and cookies, and is often sifted over desserts to add sweetness or cover blemishes.

Brown sugar, which gets its distinctive character from molasses, adds golden color and rich flavor to baked goods. The extra moisture tends to give cookies a chewy texture.

You might not look to your local farmers' market to purchase flour, but Don Lewis of Wild Hive Farm in Clinton Corners, New York, would like you to think twice about that. Lewis started out as a beekeeper (thus the farm's name) and then began baking. When he tried to source local grains for his new pursuit, he became frustrated and soon decided to grow them himself. Now, he micromills his homegrown organic grains in his garage to use in his small bakery operation. The surplus—various types of freshly milled organic flour and cornmeal—and his bakery products are sold by his son Matt at farmers' markets. The elder Lewis has been known to tote his mobile wood-fired hearth oven along to the markets to educate the community. Next up: he is working on reviving heritage grains.

Use light (golden) brown sugar for less color and molasses flavor, dark brown for more. How tightly brown sugar is packed into a measuring cup or spoon affects the quantity, so be careful to note whether a recipe specifies gently or firmly packed. Finally, the large, golden crystals of turbinado or Demerara sugar are perfect for adding sparkle to finished desserts.

VANILLA | Use pure vanilla extract, rather than imitation vanilla extract, for the finest flavor. Bourbon and Tahitian are among the most popular types, each with its own distinctive aroma and flavor profile. When using whole beans, select ones that are moist and pliable. Some recipes call for splitting a bean lengthwise, scraping the seeds into whatever is being prepared, and then adding the pod halves as well. When the spent pod halves are removed from the mixture, rinse them well, leave them to air dry, and then slip them into a jar of sugar to lend a delicate perfume. If you have used the whole bean without splitting it, rinse and dry it well, store it in an airtight jar at cool room temperature, and use it again for another recipe. It will still impart flavor.

Tips and Techniques

Many people state with great authority that baking is a science, that you cannot play around with recipes. If you are baking professionally, that's true. You must follow certain rules for perfect, reliable results. But most of us home bakers don't need every dessert to be picture-perfect or to be exactly the same as it was the last time. Instead, we are looking for something delicious, homemade, soulful. And we want to have fun making it.

The recipes in this book came about not from strict adherence to rules and formulas, but rather from experimentation inspired by the market. Without that kind of experimentation, who would have guessed to bake beets and zucchini into a chocolate cake for supreme moistness, to use a bit of gelatin to turn liquid cream into a softly set panna cotta, to bake berries into a buckle one day and a cobbler the next?

I am not suggesting that technique doesn't make a difference. Where it is especially important, I share what you need to know to get the best result. But I also let you know where you can fudge a little. You may prefer to try out your experiments on family and forgiving friends rather than on dinner guests. Although I haven't included the "mistakes" of my trial-and-error approach, most of them found enthusiastic fans happy to devour them. Life is all about balance, and here it is the balance between precision and fun that ensures you will have a great time both making and eating the desserts included in this book.

That said, a few guidelines can help you to create desserts as impressive to look at as they are delicious to eat and fun to make.

GETTING STARTED | It cannot be said often enough: carefully read through the *entire* recipe before you begin in order to be sure you have all the ingredients and tools on hand and the time available to complete important steps that cannot be postponed. It's no fun to find you are missing an ingredient or piece of equipment halfway through a recipe, or that you have to run out to a meeting when your cheesecake needs another half hour in the oven.

Always preheat the oven for at least 30 minutes before baking to give it time to reach and maintain the proper temperature. That "ding" of the oven bell isn't always reliable. Unless otherwise specified, use room-temperature ingredients (68° to 72°F) to ensure optimal blending of ingredients and incorporation of air. Remove eggs, butter, and other dairy products from the refrigerator about 30 minutes before you need them. If you have forgotten the eggs, you can warm them quickly by immersing them in a bowl of tepid water for a few minutes.

Don't forget your *mise en place*: Set out all the ingredients and equipment you will need before you begin. If the recipe calls for ½ cup blanched almonds, toasted and finely chopped, don't wait to toast them until you hit that part of the recipe. Get everything set up first and you will feel like Julia Child when you are making the recipe.

Work quickly, especially if the recipe says you should. For example, a batter can begin to separate if it stands, which can make your cake heavy or allow any fruits to fall to the bottom. As soon as the batter is mixed, get it right into the oven.

MEASURING FLOUR | When sifting flour, always measure it first, unless the recipe indicates otherwise. Use the scoop-and-sweep method for accurate measurement: Fluff the flour with a spoon, lightly spoon it into a measuring cup until overflowing, then sweep the back of a knife across the top of the cup to even it. This is one detail worth getting right: too little flour can prevent a batter from setting correctly; too much flour can produce a dry, heavy cake.

BEATING EGG WHITES | Always beat egg whites in an impeccably clean bowl with clean beaters. If the recipe calls for soft peaks, look for a rounded peak that doesn't hold its shape when you pull out the beater. Medium peaks should be smooth and a little shiny, and will gently hold their shape with the tip curled over. Firm peaks will stand up straight without drooping but should not be at all dry or separated. It is safer to stop a little early than to overbeat egg whites, which can cause them to collapse when folded into a batter and baked. When overbeating is a concern, I call for medium-firm peaks, which means you should stop beating just past medium and a little short of firm peaks.

WHIPPING CREAM | For the best volume, use very cold cream and refrigerate the bowl and beaters for 10 minutes before whipping. If a recipe calls for soft peaks, the whipped cream should not quite hold its shape. Medium peaks hold their shape softly. Firm peaks hold their shape very well. Medium-firm peaks are just beyond medium but not quite firm. For topping desserts, cream whipped to medium or medium-firm peaks has the richest, creamiest feel in the mouth.

MELTING CHOCOLATE | The safest way to melt chocolate is in a double boiler over gently simmering water. It is ready if, when you stir it, it is perfectly smooth. Unless otherwise indicated in the recipe, avoid getting moisture of any kind—including steam—into the chocolate as it melts or it will seize up, becoming stiff and grainy. Chocolate can also be melted in a microwave oven. Put coarsely chopped chocolate into a microwave-safe bowl and heat at 50 percent power for 1 minute, then check it. Even if it looks like it is in individual pieces, stir it with a silicone spatula. It may already be melted, or there may be sufficient residual heat to melt the rest. If not, microwave 30 seconds more, stir, and continue to heat and stir in 15- to 30-second increments until the chocolate is smooth.

JUDGING DONENESS | Many factors affect cooking and baking times, so a variety of alternative indicators are included in the recipes. Always check for doneness a little before the suggested time has elapsed, then decide how much more time is needed. For even baking, rotate pans front to back and, if you have pans on two different racks, switch them between the racks, about halfway through the baking time. If a dessert is browning too quickly but is not yet done, drape a piece of aluminum foil over the top or reduce the temperature by 25 degrees.

Use an oven thermometer to determine if your oven is heating accurately. Place the thermometer in the oven, set the oven to 350°F, and check the thermometer 15 minutes after the oven has finished preheating. If the oven temperature does not match the preset temperature, make a note of the difference and adjust the setting accordingly the next time you bake. If you don't have a thermometer but suspect your oven runs hot, reduce the recipe temperature by 25 degrees; if it runs cool, increase it by 25 degrees, and then continue to adjust as needed until you understand your oven's temperament.

FREEZING FRESH FRUIT | Don't let the opportunity pass to tuck away some of your favorite fruits when they are in season and perfectly ripe. If you purchase more than you can use, or if what you have purchased is threatening to turn the corner from ripe to rotten, freeze it for future use. (Avoid freezing fruit that is bruised or past its prime.) The best method is what the food industry calls IQF, or individually quick frozen. Remove the pits from stone fruits, cut into wedges, and lay them in a single layer on a rimmed baking sheet lined with parchment paper. Freeze until hard, then pack the fruit into zipper-top bags and freeze for up to 4 months. Pit cherries but leave them whole, then freeze and pack in the same manner. Berries can be quick frozen the same way, but skip rinsing them first to keep them at their best. The cell walls of fruits break down in the freezer, making the fruits mushy, so frozen fruits are better cooked than raw. For most recipes, use the frozen fruits without thawing, increasing the baking time to reach the desired doneness indicated in the recipe.

TOASTING NUTS | Spread nuts in a single layer on a rimmed baking sheet and toast them in a preheated 325°F oven until they are fragrant and have taken on color, about 12 minutes. To test, carefully cut or bite into a nut. It should be lightly golden in the center and have a toasty flavor. To remove the skins from hazelnuts, transfer the hot toasted nuts to a bowl and cover for 5 minutes, then pour them out onto a terry-cloth tea towel and rub vigorously to remove most of the skins. (Don't worry about the stubborn ones.) You can toast small quantities of nuts in a cast-iron skillet on the stove top over medium-low heat. Watch carefully and stir occasionally, as they can go quickly from toasted to burnt. Immediately transfer the toasted nuts to a heatproof surface to stop the cooking.

MASTER RECIPES

MAKE YOUR OWN CRÈME FRAÎCHE

MAKES

1

CUP

Crème fraîche is a thick, cultured cream with a pleasantly tangy flavor. It is wonderful poured over desserts that cry out for ice cream or whipped cream. It also whips well. Considering the cost of purchasing it and the ease of making it yourself, you may prefer the latter. You will need to think ahead, however. The process takes 24 to 48 hours, including chilling.

Although you may not have access to the cultures used to make proper crème fraîche, you can make a very good substitute using a good-quality yogurt or buttermilk with live, active cultures. Use the freshest, best-quality cream you can find, preferably free of emulsifiers and additives and not ultra-pasteurized. If you have purchased crème fraîche on hand, add a tablespoon of it along with the buttermilk to speed development with its crème fraîche cultures.

1 cup heavy cream
2 tablespoons cultured buttermilk or plain yogurt with live, active cultures

Combine the cream and the buttermilk in a clean glass jar. Cover, shake briefly, and leave at room temperature (70° to 75°F) for 24 to 36 hours, checking every 4 to 8 hours after the first 8 hours. It is ready when the texture is thick but still pourable with the consistency of sour cream and the taste is refreshingly tangy. Cover tightly, shake well, and refrigerate. It will continue to thicken and develop flavor during the first 24 hours or so of chilling, and should keep, covered and refrigerated, for 10 days to 2 weeks.

TANGY WHIPPED CREAM

MAKES ABOUT

2

CUPS

You can use this cream any time you would use ordinary whipped cream. It has a lot more character.

½ cup heavy cream, cold
½ cup crème fraîche, mascarpone cheese, or sour cream, cold
2 teaspoons Baker's Sugar or granulated sugar
Pinch of kosher salt
½ teaspoon pure vanilla extract or other flavoring (optional)

Using a chilled bowl and a chilled whisk or beaters, whip together the cream, crème fraîche, sugar, and salt until the mixture holds medium to medium-firm peaks. Stir in the vanilla. Refrigerate, tightly covered, for up to 3 days. Whisk briefly to smooth the cream before using.

It's hard to outdo nature's recipe for peaches: stand over the sink, prepare to get messy, and bite through the baby-cheek fuzz to the taste-of-summer juicy, fragrant flesh, leaving behind only the stony pit as evidence of your indulgence. Ask the farmers at your local market, and nine times out of ten that will be their favorite way to enjoy their tree-ripened wares.

Still, it is difficult to ask the six guests gathered around your dining table to join you in the kitchen with napkins tucked beneath their chins. Besides, what better way to complement bright, sweet peaches, plums, nectarines, apricots, and cherries than by cloaking them in pastry, churning them into ice cream, grilling or roasting them to bring out even more complex flavors, folding them into cupcake batter, or pureeing them into a simple soup?

New varieties of stone fruits are being developed all the time, taking their place alongside the traditional O'Henry peach, Santa Rosa plum, and Bing cherry. At the height of the season, I might find Flavorcrest, Indian Blood, and Saturn peaches; Arctic Star and Juneglo nectarines; Elephant Heart and Green Gage plums; and August Glo and Perfection apricots, among dozens of others, all cut up for tasting. Heirloom varieties are

being revived as well, though sadly many—like the luscious Royal Blenheim apricot—remain in short supply because they are easily bruised in transit.

Cherries have a short season, so grab them while you can. Look for Brooks and Tulare early in the season, followed by the dark purple Bing, the classic sweet cherry. Light-skinned Queen Anne and Rainier cherries are typically juicy and sweet with a hint of tartness. Sour cherries, primarily Montmorency or Morello varieties, have a very short season and aren't meant for eating raw. Cooked and sweetened, however, nothing compares to their sweet-tart complexity.

Brand-new stone fruits are turning up, too. Pluots and Apriums are hybrids of apricots and plums, with the Pluot predominantly plum with a hint of apricot and the Aprium just the opposite. Like plums, Pluots range in color from pink and red to dark purple to green, with flesh from light to dark. Names like Flavor Grenade, Dapple Fire, Yummy Giant, and Flavorella entice, but the best way to choose is to taste and track your own

"Farmer Al" Courchesne of Frog Hollow Farm and Bakery in Brentwood, California, attributes the outstanding quality of the organic stone fruits grown on this family farm to the varieties cultivated, the *terroir* of the 120-acre property, and the philosophy of picking fruit only after it has completely ripened. That can sometimes lead to waste, but the Courchesnes make use of fruit that doesn't look perfect—but still tastes great—by drying it, using it in their on-site bakery, or by cooking up jams and preserves.

favorites. The hybrids are typically sweeter than either of their parents, but most still have enough acidity for good balance.

Selecting and Storing Stone Fruits

Choose peaches, nectarines, and apricots with no tinge of green in the background. They should be fragrant and yield slightly to a gentle press of the finger. (Please don't leave behind a trail of damaged fruit!) Whether peaches are yellow or rose isn't important. The color is dictated by the variety. White-fleshed peaches and nectarines are best enjoyed raw, as they lose much of their delicate flavor when cooked. For recipes calling for fruits cut into halves or into neat slices, look for freestone fruits, which release their pits easily.

The best plums, Pluots, and cherries are more difficult to gauge. Look for firm, shiny fruits with minimal blemishes and ask for a taste. Peaches, nectarines, plums, apricots, Apriums, and Pluots have the best flavor at room temperature. Once ripe, they can be refrigerated for a few days.

Deborah Olson, fourth-generation proprietor of C. J. Olson Cherries in Sunnyvale, California, recommends discarding any bruised cherries before storing the rest unwashed in an airtight container in the coldest part of the refrigerator for up to a week. To remove stains from pitting and cutting cherries, Olson suggests squeezing a cut lemon over your hands. For stained clothing, pretreat with a stain-removing spray and be sure to wash in cold water.

APRIUM ALMOND TART

MAKES

8-10

SERVINGS

I created this tart crust when I ran out of flour after starting to make the dough for a Thanksgiving apple tart. Crossing my fingers, I substituted almond meal for half of the flour. It was a big hit. When I ran out of almond meal the next time I made it, I substituted cornmeal for part of the almond meal. Now it's just right. This tart has a distinct almond flavor from the almond paste, which balances perfectly with the Apriums.

SEASON TO TASTE: If Apriums aren't available, substitute apricots. Whether apricot or Aprium, the fruit should be ripe but not squishy soft. This tart also adapts well to other fruits, such as plums, pears (peeled, cored, and placed cut-side down on the filling), or thinly sliced tart apples, such as Gravensteins.

CRUST

1 cup unbleached all-purpose flour

⅔ cup almond meal

⅓ cup fine stone-ground yellow cornmeal

3 tablespoons granulated sugar

½ teaspoon kosher salt

½ cup (1 stick) unsalted butter, cold, cut into 8 pieces

1 large egg, lightly beaten

FILLING

½ cup (5 ounces) almond paste

2 large eggs

½ teaspoon pure vanilla extract

¼ teaspoon kosher salt

4 tablespoons (½ stick) unsalted butter, softened

CONTINUED >

1. To make the crust, put the flour, almond meal, cornmeal, sugar, and salt in a food processor and pulse a few times to mix. Scatter the butter over the top and pulse until the mixture looks like coarse meal. Add the egg and process just until the dough begins to clump around the blade.

2. Transfer the dough to a 10-inch tart pan with a removable bottom, breaking it into pieces and distributing it evenly around the pan. Using your hands or the bottom of a water glass dipped in flour, press the dough to cover the bottom and sides evenly. Place the pan on a rimless baking sheet, loosely cover with plastic film, and refrigerate for at least 30 minutes or up to overnight.

3. Preheat the oven to 375°F, with a rack in the upper third.

4. To make the filling, crumble the almond paste into the food processor and process until it is the texture of sand. (If the almond paste is hard, chop or coarsely grate it first.) Add the eggs, vanilla, and salt and process until smooth. Add the butter and process just until smooth, stopping and scraping down the bowl of the processor as needed. Add the flour and pulse just until combined.

5. Spread the almond filling over the bottom of the pastry. Stand the Aprium halves, cut-side up, on the filling, leaning one against the next in overlapping, concentric circles, like a fallen stack of dominoes. (If

CONTINUED >

2 tablespoons unbleached all-purpose flour

2½ pounds Apriums (about 25 small to medium), halved and pitted

⅓ cup apricot jam, melted over low heat, or 2 tablespoons granulated sugar, for glazing

the Apriums are 2 inches or larger, cut them into quarters and place them cut-side down on the filling.)

6. Bake for 35 minutes, then remove from the oven and raise the heat to 400°F. Brush the Apriums with the melted jam. Alternatively, sprinkle the granulated sugar evenly over the fruit, taking care to avoid the pastry. Return the tart to the oven and bake until the Apriums are glazed and tinged with brown in spots, about 15 minutes longer. Let cool on a wire rack for at least 45 minutes.

7. Center the cooled tart on a glass or small bowl to allow the outer ring to fall away. Transfer the tart, still on the pan base, to a serving plate. Alternatively, use a large metal spatula or rimless baking sheet to slide the tart from its base onto the plate. Serve slightly warm or at room temperature.

8. Refrigerate leftover tart, tightly covered, for up to 3 days. Bring to room temperature before serving.

∾ FARM JOURNAL ∾

Apriums, an apricot-plum hybrid, are meatier than plums and juicier and sweeter than most apricots, with more complex flavor. The Honey Rich variety is worth seeking out for its big flavor. Flavor Delight and Tasty Rich are also good choices.

Almond meal, sometimes called almond flour, is made by finely grinding raw, usually blanched, almonds. Bob's Red Mill brand almond meal is widely distributed in supermarkets and is often available in health food stores and at Trader Joe's locations. You can make your own almond meal by processing blanched almonds in a food processor, watching carefully to avoid making almond butter. (Freezing the almonds before grinding helps protect against this happening.)

Almond paste is made by sweetening finely ground almonds. It is available in 7-ounce tubes in the baking section of most supermarkets, or in bulk in upscale groceries and baking supply shops. It contains more almonds and less sugar than marzipan.

MAKES

4

SERVINGS

This variation on a classic French dessert is a simple way to transform a piece of fruit into a special occasion. Use freestone peaches for the prettiest dessert, as the flesh can be easily pulled from the stone in one piece. The skin lends the roasted peach a rosy hue, and it's much easier to pull off after the fruit has softened. You may not use all the raspberry sauce; refrigerate any remaining sauce in an airtight container for up to 3 days.

SEASON TO TASTE: Substitute nectarines or plums for the peaches. If the plums are small, you may want to use a few more of them.

2 tablespoons unsalted butter

2 tablespoons firmly packed light or dark brown sugar

Small pinch of kosher salt

4 small to medium or 2 large, firm-ripe peaches, halved and pitted

RASPBERRY SAUCE

1 pint (about 2 cups) raspberries

¼ cup granulated sugar

3 tablespoons raspberry liqueur (optional)

1 pint premium vanilla ice cream

1. Preheat the oven to 400°F, with a rack in the upper third.

2. Melt the butter in a large cast-iron or other ovenproof skillet over medium heat. Sprinkle the brown sugar and salt evenly over the butter and heat until bubbly, about 2 minutes. Briefly stir or swirl the butter and sugar, then put the peaches, cut-side down, into the skillet and cook for 3 minutes longer. Transfer the skillet to the oven and roast the fruit until it is quite tender when pierced with a knife but not falling apart, about 25 minutes.

3. Return the pan to the stove top to cool. When the fruit is cool enough to handle, use a paring knife or the back of a spoon to coax off the skin; it should pull off easily. (Swirled in the warm pan juices for a moment, the skin makes a wonderful cook's treat!) Spoon some of the pan juices over the peaches as they cool.

4. To make the raspberry sauce, stir the raspberries and sugar in a small saucepan over medium heat until the berries release their juices and begin to fall apart, about 3 minutes. Put through a fine-mesh strainer into a bowl, stirring and pushing against the strainer to extract as much of the pulp as possible, leaving the seeds behind. Stir in the raspberry liqueur (if using).

5. Place two large or four smaller, barely warm peach halves, cut-side up, in each shallow serving bowl. Spoon the pan juices over them. Top each peach half with a scoop of ice cream. Pour the raspberry sauce over the ice cream, and serve any remaining sauce in a pitcher on the table.

NECTARINE-BLUEBERRY COBBLER

MAKES

6–8

SERVINGS

Some say the cobbler got its name because the dessert is cobbled together from whatever is available to the cook. Others believe the biscuit topping suggests a cobblestone walkway. Whatever the origin, it's an easy and delicious way to use your favorite fruits.

Cherry concentrate is made from 100 percent fruit, typically either black (sweet) cherries or tart cherries, and is meant to be diluted for drinking. It is available in the frozen- or bottled-juice section of many supermarkets, specialty food stores, a nd natural food stores. If you use a concentrate made from tart cherries, increase the sugar in the filling to ¾ cup.

SEASON TO TASTE : Substitute other stone fruits, such as peaches, apricots, or plums, for the nectarines, or use blackberries or olallieberries in place of the blueberries. Keeping to just two types of fruit ensures the distinctive flavor of each will shine through.

FILLING

½ cup bottled cherry concentrate or thawed frozen cherry concentrate

¼ cup quick-cooking tapioca

½ cup granulated sugar

2 teaspoons fresh lemon juice

4 to 6 firm-ripe nectarines (about 2 pounds), peeled, pitted, and cut into ½-inch-thick slices

1 pint (2 cups) blueberries, stems removed

BISCUIT TOPPING

1½ cups unbleached all-purpose flour

2 tablespoons granulated sugar

1 teaspoon baking powder

¼ teaspoon baking soda

¼ teaspoon kosher salt

1. Preheat the oven to 400°F, with a rack in the lower third. Butter a 9-inch square baking pan.

2. To make the filling, stir together the cherry concentrate, tapioca, sugar, and lemon juice in a bowl. Add the nectarines and blueberries and toss to coat evenly. Turn the fruit into the prepared baking pan.

3. To make the topping, stir together the flour, sugar, baking powder, baking soda, and salt in a bowl. Scatter the butter over the top. Using a pastry blender, two knives, or your fingertips, cut in the butter until it is in pieces that vary in size from oat flakes to peas. Drizzle the buttermilk over the mixture and toss with a fork or your fingers just until combined.

4. Transfer the mixture to a lightly floured work surface and knead gently 2 or 3 times to form a soft dough. Pat the dough into a ½-inch-thick round. Using a floured drinking glass or cookie cutter about 3 inches in diameter, cut out round (or other shape) biscuits. For the best rise, cut straight down without twisting.

5. Arrange the biscuits over the fruit to cover most of the surface, with only small spaces between the biscuits. Sprinkle the turbinado sugar evenly over the biscuits.

6 tablespoons unsalted butter, cold,
cut into 6 pieces

⅔ cup buttermilk

2 tablespoons turbinado, Demerara, or
other coarse sugar

Lemon Verbena Buttermilk Ice Cream
(page 197; without the berry sauce)
or premium vanilla ice cream, for
serving (optional)

6. Bake until the biscuits are golden and the fruit is bubbling enthusiastically, 35 to 40 minutes. Let cool in the pan for at least 15 minutes before serving. Serve warm or at room temperature, topped with ice cream.

7. Refrigerate leftover cobbler, tightly covered, for up to 2 days. Place in a preheated 350°F oven to warm the fruit and crisp the biscuit tops before serving.

MAKES

6–8

SERVINGS

Sweet-tart plums are a perfect complement to the caramel in this French dessert, which is traditionally made with apples. Caramel doesn't need to be intimidating, but it does get wickedly hot. Be prepared with a steady hand and good oven mitts. You'll need an 11-inch ovenproof skillet, 1½ to 2 inches deep. A cast-iron skillet works well; a nonstick skillet does not. The pastry for the crust can be mixed in advance.

SEASON TO TASTE: Substitute peaches, apricots, pears, or apples for the plums. For pears and apples, which need to cook longer than plums, reduce the oven temperature to 350°F and bake for 45 to 60 minutes.

CRUST

1¼ cups unbleached all-purpose flour

1 tablespoon granulated sugar

¼ teaspoon kosher salt

½ cup (1 stick) unsalted butter, cold, cut into 8 pieces

About 3 tablespoons ice-cold sparkling water

PLUMS

4 tablespoons (½ stick) unsalted butter

¾ cup granulated sugar

¼ teaspoon kosher salt

2 pounds firm-ripe plums (8 to 10 medium), halved and pitted (or quartered if large)

Premium vanilla ice cream; lightly sweetened, softly whipped cream; or Tangy Whipped Cream (page 27), for serving (optional)

1. To make the crust, put the flour, sugar, and salt in a food processor and pulse a few times to mix. Scatter the butter pieces over the top and pulse until the mixture resembles coarse meal. With the motor running, slowly drizzle in the sparkling water, a little at a time, adding just enough for the dough to begin clumping around the blade.

2. Transfer the dough to a lightly floured work surface and, without handling more than necessary, flatten it into a disk. Wrap in plastic film and refrigerate for at least 30 minutes or up to 2 days.

3. While the dough rests, prepare the plums. Combine the butter, sugar, and salt in a heavy, ovenproof 11-by-2-inch skillet over medium-low heat. As the butter melts, stir to moisten the sugar. Then leave the sugar to melt, stirring only occasionally, until it begins to turn amber, 4 to 6 minutes. If the sugar and butter separate, stir with flat whisk until you once again have a smooth mixture, taking care not to slosh the butter.

4. Remove the pan from the heat and, keeping in mind that the pan and caramel are sizzling hot, carefully arrange the plums, cut-side up, in tightly packed, concentric circles over the caramel, using as many plums as will fit. Set the pan aside off the heat.

5. Preheat the oven to 400°F, with a rack near the center.

6. Place the dough disk between two sheets of lightly floured plastic film and roll out into an 11½-inch circle. Peel off the top sheet and use

the bottom sheet to flip the circle over the plums. Carefully peel off the second sheet of plastic film. Use a silicone spatula to tuck the pastry inside the rim of the pan around the fruit. Use a paring knife to cut four small vents in the pastry.

7. Bake until the crust is a rich golden brown, about 30 minutes. Use oven mitts to transfer the skillet carefully to the stove top to cool for 20 minutes.

8. To unmold the tart, invert a 12- to 13-inch platter over the skillet. Using oven mitts, grasp the plate and skillet tightly together on both sides and quickly invert the plate and skillet to release the tart onto the plate. Lift off the skillet, scraping any remaining caramelized juices from the pan over the tart, and adjust any plums that may have slipped out of position. Serve wedges of the tart warm or at room temperature, topped with ice cream.

9. Store leftover tart, tightly covered, at room temperature for up to 2 days. Reheat on a baking sheet in a preheated 375°F oven for about 10 minutes before serving, if desired.

∾ FARM JOURNAL ๑

More than 140 plum varieties are sold in the United States, about 20 of which are widely available. The rest are limited to backyard trees and farmers' markets. They range from the size of a cherry to a small peach, with yellow, green, or inky dark skin and yellow to crimson flesh. In this tart, Simka Rosa plums shine with their deep red skin and sweet-tart cranberry flavor. Sweet, dark Santa Rosa plums also work well, as will other types that remain somewhat firm when ripe.

DEEP-DISH SOUR CHERRY PIE

MAKES

10

SERVINGS

This rustic, sweet-tart galette is baked in a pie pan to make room for plenty of cherries and not a whole lot more. A cherry pitter comes in handy, and my favorite is the Push Button Cherry Pitter developed by a tool and die maker in Sturgeon Bay, Wisconsin (see page 20).

SEASON TO TASTE: You can substitute sweet cherries for the sour ones, though the flavor will be quite different. If you do, reduce the sugar in the filling to 1 cup and add 1 tablespoon fresh lemon juice. Adapt this recipe to other fruits, such as peaches or plums, by adjusting the sugar and tapioca in the filling according to the sweetness and juiciness of the fruit.

CRUST

1½ cups unbleached all-purpose flour

1 tablespoon granulated sugar

½ teaspoon kosher salt

½ cup (1 stick) unsalted butter, cold, cut into 8 pieces

2 ounces cream cheese, cold

About 2 tablespoons ice water

FILLING

2½ pounds sour cherries, pitted (about 8 cups)

1⅓ cups granulated sugar

¼ cup unbleached all-purpose flour

1 tablespoon tapioca starch, or 2 tablespoons quick-cooking tapioca

½ teaspoon kosher salt

1 tablespoon unsalted butter, cut into small pieces

1 tablespoon heavy cream, half-and-half, or milk

1. To make the crust, put the flour, sugar, and salt in a food processor and pulse a few times to mix. Scatter the butter over the top and pulse until the butter is in pea-size pieces. Break the cream cheese into three or four pieces and add to the food processor. Pulse until the butter and cream cheese are in pieces that vary in size from oat flakes to peas. With the motor running, slowly drizzle in the water, a little at a time, adding just enough for the dough to hold together when you pinch a clump between your fingers. Listen for the sound of the motor to deepen, a clue that the dough is ready.

2. Turn the dough out onto a work surface, gather it into a ball, cover with a tea towel, and let rest for 15 minutes. (Alternatively, wrap the ball with plastic film and refrigerate for up to 1 day, then let rest at room temperature for 15 minutes before rolling.)

3. Preheat the oven to 400°F, with a rack in the upper third and a rimless baking sheet centered on the rack.

4. Place the dough disk between two sheets of lightly floured plastic film and roll out into a 14-inch circle. Peel off the top sheet and use the bottom one to flip the circle over a 10-by-2-inch deep-dish pie pan, fitting it snugly but gently into the pan without stretching or pressing it and with an even overhang around the rim. Carefully loosen the second sheet of plastic film and refrigerate.

5. To make the filling, stir the cherries, sugar, flour, tapioca, and salt in a large, wide saucepan over medium-high heat until the juices

About 2 tablespoons turbinado, Demerara, or other coarse sugar

bubble and begin to thicken, about 5 minutes. Pour the cherries and all the juices into the pastry-lined pan and spread evenly. Dot the cherries all over with the butter. Fold the pastry overhang up and over the cherries, tucking and pleating the pastry to form a wide rim that snugly fits over the fruit. Brush the pastry with the cream, and sprinkle the turbinado sugar over the pastry and the fruit.

6. Place the pie pan on the preheated baking sheet and bake for 20 minutes. Reduce the oven temperature to 350°F, rotate the pan front to back, and bake until the pastry is golden and the filling is bubbling enthusiastically, about 25 minutes longer. (If the pastry begins to brown too quickly, cover it with strips of aluminum foil.) Let cool on a wire rack for at least 2 hours before serving.

7. Refrigerate leftover pie, tightly covered, for up to 3 days. Bring to room temperature or place in a preheated 350°F oven just until warm before serving.

～ FARM JOURNAL ～

The fact that these sour fruits are often referred to as pie cherries says it all: sour cherries rule when it comes to making pies. The two most common varieties are Montmorency, the predominant sour cherry in the United States, and Morello, which is more common in Europe. Sugar and heat transform the sour fruits into firm-textured orbs with an intoxicating flavor that balances sweet and sour.

Montmorency cherries are smaller and brighter red than their sweet cousins. And although they are very juicy raw, and give up quite a bit of juice as they cook, they remain firmer than sweet cherries after baking. The ruby fruits with yellow flesh are easiest to pit when they are chilled. They are quite fragile and bruise easily, so handle them gingerly and use them within a day or two of picking. Their short season runs for just a couple of weeks around the beginning of July, and you won't find them just anywhere: Michigan, Utah, and Washington are the major commercial growers, but they are also grown in Oregon, Wisconsin, New York, and California.

MAKES

8

SERVINGS

I was beaming when my pie took first prize in the San Francisco Professional Food Society's 1997 peach pie contest, the year I joined. I had spent weeks refining the recipe to get the proportions of filling to crust right, the crust flaky, and the filling to hold together with just the right type and amount of starch. That recipe sacrificed some flavor in the name of flakiness by using part vegetable shortening. The farmers' market spirit dictates all butter, however, which ensures a rich, flavorful crust. A bit of vinegar keeps it tender—you won't taste it.

More than anything, the success of the pie depends on the quality of the peaches. Select fruit that is juicy and flavorful. Peaches with a tinge of red in the flesh make a beautifully rosy filling.

CRUST

2 cups unbleached all-purpose flour

½ cup whole-wheat pastry flour

1 tablespoon firmly packed light brown sugar

1 teaspoon kosher salt

1 cup (2 sticks) unsalted butter, cold, cut into 16 pieces

2 teaspoons distilled white vinegar

2 to 4 tablespoons ice water

FILLING

3 pounds ripe but not squishy peaches (about 12 medium), halved, pitted, and sliced

1 lemon, preferably Meyer

¾ cup granulated sugar

½ teaspoon kosher salt

2 tablespoons tapioca starch, or 3 tablespoons quick-cooking tapioca

CONTINUED >

1. To make the crust, put the all-purpose flour, pastry flour, brown sugar, and salt in a food processor and pulse a few times to mix. Scatter the butter over the top and pulse until the mixture looks like coarse meal. Stir together the vinegar and 2 tablespoons of the ice water in a small bowl. Sprinkle the vinegar mixture over the flour mixture a little at a time, pulsing briefly after each addition, until the dough just holds together when you press it gently with your fingers. Add the remaining ice water as needed to achieve the correct consistency.

2. Transfer the dough to a lightly floured work surface and, without handling more than necessary, flatten it into two disks, one slightly larger than the other. Wrap the disks separately in plastic film and refrigerate for at least 4 hours or up to overnight.

3. Remove the disks from the refrigerator. Preheat the oven to 425°F, with a rack near the center.

4. To make the filling, put about half of the peach slices into a heavy saucepan and the other half in a large bowl. Grate ½ teaspoon zest from the lemon and add to the peaches in the pan, along with the granulated sugar, salt, and tapioca. Place the pan over medium heat and stir gently until the sugar, salt, and tapioca are completely dissolved and the peaches begin to give up a little juice, about 2 minutes. When the juices just begin to bubble and thicken, remove the pan from the heat and transfer the contents to the bowl holding the

CONTINUED >

GLAZE

1 egg, lightly beaten with 1 tablespoon half-and-half

1 tablespoon turbinado, Demerara, or other coarse sugar

remaining peach slices. Halve the lemon, squeeze 2 teaspoons juice from it, and add to the peaches. Toss to coat evenly. Set aside to cool while you roll out the pastry.

5. Place the dough disk between two sheets of lightly floured plastic film and roll out into a 12-inch circle. Peel off the top sheet and use the bottom sheet to flip the circle into a 9-by-2-inch deep-dish pie pan, fitting it gently into the pan without stretching or pressing it. Carefully peel off and set aside the second sheet of plastic film. Trim the edges to leave a 1/2-inch overhang. Refrigerate, loosely covered with plastic film.

6. Roll the remaining disk between two sheets of lightly floured plastic film into a 10-inch circle, again with a floured pin. Distribute the peaches evenly in the bottom crust. Paint the edges of the crust with a bit of the egg wash. (Save the rest for later.) Transfer the 10-inch circle the same way you moved the bottom crust, centering it over the filled pie. Tuck the edges of the top circle under the overhang of the bottom crust to make a tight seal. Crimp with a fork or your fingers to create an edge on the rim of the pan. With a paring knife, cut a few decorative vents near the center of the top crust. Brush the top crust with the remaining egg wash (you may not use all of it) and sprinkle with the coarse sugar.

7. Place the pie on a rimmed baking sheet and transfer to the oven. Bake for 15 minutes, then reduce the oven temperature to 375°F and bake until the crust is a rich, golden brown, about 50 minutes longer. Let cool on a wire rack for at least 1 hour before serving.

8. Refrigerate leftover pie, tightly covered, for up to 3 days. Bring to room temperature or heat in a preheated 350°F oven just until warm before serving.

EASY CHOCOLATE CHERRY CUPCAKES

MAKES

12

CUPCAKES

These cupcakes aren't just easy. They are also moist, light, chocolaty, and irresistible. The frosting, adapted from a recipe by the late James Beard, is one of the easiest and best I know. Use a sour cream without a lot of added gums, which can affect the texture of the frosting. Light-skinned, blushing Queen Anne or Rainier cherries make the prettiest toppers.

CUPCAKES

36 firm-ripe cherries, at least 12 with stems

1 tablespoon kirsch

1⅓ cups unbleached all-purpose flour

1 cup granulated sugar

¼ cup unsweetened natural cocoa powder (not Dutch processed)

1 teaspoon baking soda

½ teaspoon kosher salt

¾ cup plus 2 tablespoons cold water

5 tablespoons canola oil

1 teaspoon distilled white vinegar

¾ teaspoon pure vanilla extract

FROSTING

1½ cups (9 ounces) semisweet chocolate chips

6 ounces bittersweet chocolate (60 to 70 percent cacao), chopped

1½ cups sour cream or crème fraîche, at room temperature

1½ teaspoons kirsch

1. Preheat the oven to 350°F, with a rack near the center. Line a 12-cup standard muffin tin with paper, aluminum, or silicone liners.

2. To make the cupcakes, set aside the 12 nicest cherries with stems. Stem and pit the remaining cherries and cut into halves if small, quarters if large. Toss with the kirsch. Set aside.

3. Whisk together the flour, sugar, cocoa, baking soda, and salt in a bowl. Stir in the water, oil, vinegar, and vanilla until combined. Fold in the cherries, including any juices in the bowl.

4. Scoop into the prepared liners, filling them about two-thirds full. Bake until a toothpick inserted near the center of a cupcake tests clean, about 30 minutes. Transfer the pan to a wire rack until cool enough to handle, then transfer the cupcakes directly to the rack to cool completely.

5. To make the frosting, combine the chocolate chips and the chopped chocolate in the top of a double boiler over (but not touching) gently simmering water and melt, stirring as needed, until completely melted and perfectly smooth. (Or, melt in a microwave oven.) Remove the top of the double boiler from the heat and stir in the sour cream and kirsch until well combined. Set aside to firm up until spreadable, about 20 minutes.

6. Using an icing spatula, or a pastry bag fitted with a no. 16 star tip or your preferred tip for frosting, frost the cooled cupcakes. Top each cupcake with a reserved cherry while the frosting is still soft. Serve immediately, or let stand for up to 2 hours before serving.

7. Refrigerate leftover cupcakes, tightly covered, for up to 2 days.

CHILLED PLUM SOUP WITH SOUR CREAM

MAKES

6–8

SERVINGS

One childhood role I had was to re-create my grandmother's best hits for my dad. Plum soup with sour cream, which he called by its Yiddish name, *pomella*, was one of his favorites. This grown-up version is every bit as satisfying, served in shot glasses as a sort of dessert *amuse-bouche*, or in bowls accompanied by crisp Hazelnut-Almond Biscotti (page 191), Lavender Walnut Sandies (page 194), or Market Jam Gems (page 174) made with plum jam, if you can find it. The soup is perfect for making in advance because it needs time to chill. If you have leftover soup, take a tip from recipe tester Emily Lichtenstein: freeze it in Popsicle molds for a refreshing plum pop!

Use flavorful, dark flesh plum varieties, such as Santa Rosa or Yummy Rosa, for the soup. The fruit should be quite ripe and soft but not bruised. This recipe is a great way to use up plums about to go over the hill.

SEASON TO TASTE: Try other stone fruits, such as peaches, nectarines, or cherries. Strawberries or blackberries also make a delicious soup, though you may want to strain out the seeds. Omit the cassis or substitute a complementary light-colored liqueur for light-colored fruits.

4 cups water

⅔ cup granulated sugar

¼ teaspoon kosher salt

Few twists of black pepper

2 pounds firm-ripe plums, pitted and coarsely chopped

1 sprig lemon verbena, about 4 inches long (optional)

2 tablespoons crème de cassis or other berry liqueur

½ teaspoon finely grated lemon zest

2 teaspoons fresh lemon juice

About ½ cup sour cream or crème fraîche, for serving

6 to 8 small sprigs mint or lemon verbena, for garnish

1. Combine the water, sugar, salt, and pepper in a large, heavy, nonreactive saucepan over medium-high heat and bring to a boil, stirring until the sugar is completely dissolved. Add the plums, bring back to a boil, and then reduce the heat to a gentle simmer. Skim off any foam that rises to the top, stirring occasionally, until the fruit is very soft and falling apart, about 20 minutes.

2. Remove from the heat and stir in the lemon verbena sprig (if using). Let cool for about 20 minutes, tasting occasionally and removing the lemon verbena when its flavor has perfumed the soup to your liking. It should be a delicate background note, not a predominant flavor.

3. Puree the soup until smooth using an immersion blender, standard blender, or food processor. Stir in the crème de cassis and lemon zest and juice. Cover and refrigerate until very cold, about 4 hours or up to 4 days.

4. Ladle the chilled soup into shallow bowls. Top each serving with a dollop of sour cream and a mint sprig.

A BASKET OF BERRIES

The closer to the vine, the better the berry. If you have a U-pick farm in your area, bring out the gloves (those stickers can be nasty!) and head out for the freshest, ripest berries you will ever taste. Next best is the farmers' market, where berries were usually harvested the same morning.

At the height of the berry season—from early spring through autumn—you will find deep, red strawberries; fat blackberries and boysenberries; blueberries, from tiny wild ones to jumbo size; raspberries in red, white, or black; and fragile mulberries and *fraises des bois* that rarely make it into grocery stores. This bounty is delicious raw with a little sour cream or crème fraîche and a drizzle of honey or sprinkling of sugar. Berries also brighten many desserts as a topping, providing just the right bit of acid in addition to sweetness. Mix them with a little sugar and heat gently, and they exude their fragrant juices, making simple, delicious sauces and fillings. Baked into desserts, they add vivid color and flavor.

You have to be in the right part of the country to find cranberries, the tart little orbs that hold down the late end of the berry season from September to December. Cranberries are Wisconsin's top fruit crop in both value and acreage: a $350 million industry supporting 7,200 jobs, according to the Wisconsin State Cranberry Growers Association. The state accounts for more than half of the world supply, with the remainder grown primarily in Massachusetts, New Jersey, Oregon, Washington, and British Columbia. The berries were first cultivated on a large scale in Cape Cod, which is why you may associate them with the Pilgrims and Thanksgiving.

The cranberry is one of few fruits that is a true North American native. Like blueberries (and many other fruits), they are a potent source of antioxidants and are said to provide a wide range of other health benefits. They grow on vines in bogs or marshes, which are typically flooded in the fall to set the cranberries afloat for harvest. Warrens, Wisconsin, holds the largest and oldest of the state's many cranberry festivals, with tours of working cranberry marshes and both culinary and recreational activities.

Selecting and Storing Berries

Most market vendors proudly display a basket of their berries for tasting. Work your way around the market and choose the ones that speak to you. Strawberries should be wildly fragrant when ripe. Whether large or small is a matter of variety more than quality, though the smallest ones are often sweetest. Blueberries should be plump and full, with the smallest ones often possessing the most distinctive flavor. A powdery white coating means they were recently picked. Blackberries and many of the hybrids are often juicier and more flavorful when large. Be sure to lift any baskets of berries and look underneath for mold or fruit damage.

Berries are fragile, so plan to use them quickly. Refrigerate them between layers of paper toweling in an airtight container for a couple of days. To use them, put them into a large strainer and rinse briefly under a gentle flow of cool water, shaking off any excess. Pick off and discard any stems from blueberries and cranberries. Most berries have the best flavor at room temperature.

Swanton Berry Farm grows intensely flavorful strawberries on twenty acres in Davenport, California. Before the farm got started in 1983, there were no commercially successful organic strawberries. And that is not the only ground the people at Swanton have broken: Swanton is the first U.S. organic farm to sign a contract with the United Farmworkers of America AFL-CIO. It operates with 100 percent union labor. They also make the truest strawberry jam I have ever tasted.

MAKES

4

SERVINGS

Panna cotta sounds and tastes exotic, but the cook's secret is that it's quick and easy to make. (It needs several hours to chill, however.) The Italian translation is simply "cooked cream," which is thickened into a creamy pudding with just a small amount of gelatin. Use broad, shallow molds—about 4 inches across—for the prettiest presentation.

Yogurt made from goat's milk gives this dessert a rich, complex flavor without a hint of the source. Balsamic and black pepper are natural companions of the strawberry, and fitting for this Italian dessert. Look for cream and yogurt that have no gums or additives. If goat's milk yogurt isn't available in your area, substitute Greek-style plain whole-milk yogurt. It is worth splurging on top-quality aged balsamic—the one labeled *aceto balsamico tradizionale* in Italy.

SEASON TO TASTE: Try other berry varieties in place of the strawberries.

PANNA COTTA

1¼ teaspoons unflavored gelatin

2 tablespoons water

1¼ cups heavy cream

1 cup plain goat's milk yogurt

1 teaspoon pure vanilla extract

Small pinch of sea salt or kosher salt

⅓ cup granulated sugar

TOPPING

1½ pints (about 3 cups) strawberries, hulled

1 tablespoon granulated sugar

2 teaspoons fresh lemon juice

1 to 3 tablespoons best-quality balsamic vinegar

¼ teaspoon freshly ground black pepper

Small pinch of sea salt or kosher salt

1. To make the panna cotta, sprinkle the gelatin evenly over the water in a small bowl without stirring. Let stand until softened, about 10 minutes.

2. Whisk together ½ cup of the cream, the yogurt, vanilla, and salt in a bowl, preferably with a pour spout. Gently heat the remaining ¾ cup cream with the sugar in a small saucepan over medium-low heat, stirring until the sugar is dissolved and bubbles begin to form along the edge of the pan. It should be very warm but not so hot you can't touch it.

3. Remove from the heat and, using a silicone spatula, scrape in the softened gelatin, then stir for a full minute to dissolve the gelatin completely. (Don't rush this step; it is important.) Stir the cream-gelatin mixture into the yogurt mixture.

4. Pour the mixture into four 6-ounce ramekins or custard cups, dividing it evenly. Refrigerate until set (they should be slightly jiggly but each will move as a whole), about 4 hours or up to 3 days. To avoid condensation, cover tightly with plastic film only after completely cold.

CONTINUED >

5. To make the topping, 30 to 60 minutes before serving, cut 2 ½ cups of the berries into ¼-inch-thick slices from top to tip and place in a bowl. Quarter the remaining berries and puree them with the sugar and lemon juice in a blender or food processor until smooth. Stir the puree into the sliced berries, then stir in 1 tablespoon of the balsamic vinegar, the pepper, and salt. Taste and add more sugar, balsamic, or pepper, if desired. The seasonings are meant to complement the berries, not overwhelm them. Set aside at room temperature for at least 30 minutes.

6. Run a thin, sharp knife around the inside of each ramekin, then invert onto a broad-rimmed, shallow soup bowl or dessert plate, tapping gently on the bottom of the ramekin to encourage release. If the panna cotta is stubborn, carefully insert the knife between the inverted panna cotta and the ramekin to coax it; it should slip right out. Stir the balsamic strawberries once or twice, and then spoon them and their juices over and around each panna cotta.

∾ FARM JOURNAL ∾

One of my favorite yogurts is made by Redwood Hill Farm in Sebastopol, California, where the Bice family and their farm crew call each of their happy 350 or so Nubian, Alpine, Saanen, Toggenburg, Oberhasli, and LaMancha goats by name! The sensitive, affectionate, floppy-eared Nubians produce milk with the highest butterfat, 4 to 5 percent, but they are not big producers. Pointy-eared white Saanens, on the other hand, give up lots of milk, but with only about 3 percent butterfat. Redwood Hill's strawberry goat yogurt is ribboned with a simple jam made from fresh berries, fruit juice, and honey. Yum.

STRAWBERRIES & CREAM CAKE ROLL

MAKES

8

SERVINGS

This takeoff on strawberry shortcake is elegant enough for a dinner party and, despite a few construction steps, not at all difficult to make. It can be made several hours or even a day ahead, making it perfect for entertaining.

SEASON TO TASTE: In place of the sliced strawberries, use raspberries, olallieberries, or blackberries, coarsely chopped if very large. In the filling, substitute crème de cassis for the Grand Marnier with blackberries, or raspberry liqueur with raspberries.

FILLING

2 pints (about 4 cups) strawberries, hulled

3 tablespoons granulated sugar

2 teaspoons orange liqueur, such as Grand Marnier (optional)

1 cup heavy cream

⅓ cup crème fraîche or sour cream

½ teaspoon pure vanilla extract

CAKE

5 large eggs, separated cold, then left at room temperature for at least 30 minutes

⅔ cup granulated sugar

1 teaspoon pure vanilla extract

1 cup cake flour, sifted before measuring

½ teaspoon kosher salt

Confectioners' sugar, for rolling and finishing

1. To begin the filling, set aside 1 cup of the berries for garnish. Cut the remainder into ½-inch-thick slices and toss with 2 tablespoons of the sugar and the liqueur (if using). Set aside at room temperature while you prepare the cake batter.

2. Preheat the oven to 400°F, with a rack near the center. Oil a 17-by-12-inch rimmed baking sheet and line with a silicone baking mat or parchment paper. Oil the mat or parchment.

3. To make the cake, in the bowl of a standing mixer fitted with the whisk attachment (or with a handheld mixer), beat the egg whites on medium speed until they hold soft peaks. Add ⅓ cup of the granulated sugar in a slow, steady stream, then increase the speed to medium-high and continue to beat until the whites hold medium-firm peaks. Set aside.

4. In a large bowl, using the mixer with the whisk attachment, beat together the egg yolks, vanilla, and the remaining ⅓ cup sugar on high speed until thick and pale, about 5 minutes with a standing mixer and a little longer with a handheld mixer. Stop and scrape down the bowl as needed. On low speed, mix in the flour and salt just until combined.

5. Whisk the whites briefly to bring them back to medium-firm peaks. Using a large spatula or whisk, gently fold one-third of the whites into the yolk mixture to lighten it, then fold in the remaining whites just until combined.

CONTINUED >

6. Immediately pour the batter into the prepared pan and spread evenly. Bake until the top feels dry and springs back when you press it lightly with your finger near the center, about 8 minutes. It should remain pale. Transfer the pan to a wire rack, cover with a tea towel, and let cool for 10 minutes.

7. Run a thin knife around the inside edge of the pan to loosen the cake sides. Using a fine-mesh strainer, dust the top of the cake lightly with confectioners' sugar, re-cover the cake with the towel, and invert a rimless baking sheet on top. Invert the pans together, releasing the cake onto the towel and rimless sheet. Lift off the top pan and peel off the mat or parchment. Let the cake cool completely, 20 to 30 minutes longer.

8. To complete the filling, using a chilled bowl and beaters, whip the cream, crème fraîche, vanilla, and the remaining 1 tablespoon sugar until the mixture holds firm peaks. Strain the berries, capturing their juices in a bowl, and fold the drained berries into the cream.

9. Cut the berries reserved for garnish in half, from top to tip. Mix them with the reserved berry juices.

10. Position the cake with a long side parallel to the edge of the work surface, and place a serving platter at the opposite long side. Spread the cream filling evenly over the cake, leaving a narrow border on the short sides and a 1-inch border along both long sides.

11. Starting at the long side closest to you, fold the 1-inch border tightly over the filling, then begin to roll, using the towel to help form a compact roll and pulling it out of the way as you go. Then, use the towel to help you transfer the cake, seam-side down, onto the serving platter. Use a thin or serrated sharp knife to trim just a bit from the ends of the cake to create a slight angle (baker's snack!). Refrigerate the cake, tightly covered, until very cold, about 2 hours or up to 1 day.

12. Sift confectioners' sugar over the top, and spoon the reserved berries around the base. Cut the cake with a thin or serrated sharp knife at a slight angle, using a gentle sawing motion.

∾ FARM JOURNAL ℘

If you are accustomed to shopping in a super-market, you may not know that many straw-berry varieties are cultivated, each with its own constellation of size, color, texture, and flavor. Don't discriminate against strawberries because of their size, shape, or color. Instead, follow your nose: fragrant berries are likely to be ripe and flavorful.

Chandler, Diamante, Douglas, Ogallala, Seascape, Sequoia, and Sweet Charlie varieties are particularly flavorful, with the Ogallala combining the floral aroma and flavor of wild strawberries with the larger size of domesticated (or farmed) varieties. Which are available at your market will depend on where you shop, but the farmers' market gives you the perfect chance to taste and discover the sweetest for yourself.

STRAWBERRY BUCKWHEAT TEA CAKE

MAKES

8

SERVINGS

I have been haunted by the ethereal combination of strawberries and buckwheat ever since sinking my fork into a stack of berry-studded, buckwheat-flecked pancakes at Ella's restaurant in San Francisco many years ago. This cake hits all the right notes, with sour cream to keep it moist and browned butter for that "cooked in butter" pancake flavor. Sugared strawberries and cream provide the finishing touch.

This cake is best the day it is baked. However, leftover cake may be refrigerated, tightly covered, for up to 3 days, and then brought back to room temperature before serving.

SEASON TO TASTE: Substitute other berries, a combination of berries, or sliced peaches for the strawberries. If you have rhubarb on hand, the cake is lovely with the same rhubarb sauce used for Rhubarb, Blueberry & Cream Parfait on page 147.

½ cup (1 stick) unsalted butter

1 cup unbleached all-purpose flour

½ cup buckwheat flour

¾ cup plus 1 tablespoon granulated sugar

1½ teaspoons baking powder

½ teaspoon baking soda

½ teaspoon kosher salt

½ cup sour cream or Greek-style plain whole-milk yogurt

2 large eggs

½ teaspoon pure vanilla extract

2 pints (4 cups) strawberries, hulled and cut lengthwise into ⅛- to ¼-inch-thick slices

Lightly sweetened, softly whipped cream, for serving

1. Preheat the oven to 350°F, with a rack near the center. Butter an 8-by-2-inch square baking pan or 9-by-2-inch round cake pan.

2. Melt the butter in a small skillet or saucepan over medium heat, swirling the pan once the butter has melted, until it turns a deep gold and releases a nutty aroma, 4 to 6 minutes. Pour into a heatproof bowl and let cool.

3. Whisk together the all-purpose flour, buckwheat flour, ¾ cup of the sugar, the baking powder, baking soda, and salt in a bowl. Whisk the sour cream, eggs, and vanilla into the cooled butter. Stir the butter mixture into the flour mixture just until combined. Using a spatula, gently fold in 1½ cups of the strawberries.

4. Spread the batter evenly in the prepared pan. Scatter 1 cup of the strawberries over the top. Bake until a toothpick inserted near the center (avoiding the berries) tests clean, 40 to 45 minutes. Let cool on a wire rack for at least 20 minutes.

5. While the cake bakes, toss the remaining strawberries with the 1 tablespoon sugar. Set aside at room temperature.

6. Serve the cake warm or at room temperature. Top each serving with whipped cream and some of the reserved berries.

MAKES

9

SERVINGS

You'll end up black and blue fighting over this delicious concoction! In the lexicon of old-fashioned fruit desserts, the buckle is the one with a crumb topping over fresh fruit supported by a thin layer of cake. As it bakes, the berries bubble up and the topping quakes, creating a buckled appearance.

The dessert is best served warm the day it is baked, but I would never turn down a slice for breakfast the next morning, either cold from the fridge or warm, with a little milk or cream. The topping can be made and refrigerated, tightly covered, up to 2 days ahead.

SEASON TO TASTE: Substitute any ripe berries or combination of berries for the blueberries and blackberries.

TOPPING

½ cup unbleached all-purpose flour

⅓ cup gently packed light or dark brown sugar

¼ teaspoon ground cinnamon

¼ teaspoon kosher salt

4 tablespoons (½ stick) unsalted butter, cold, cut into 4 pieces

¼ cup pecans or almonds, toasted and chopped medium-fine

FILLING

1½ cups blueberries

1½ cups blackberries

1 tablespoon granulated sugar

1 teaspoon finely grated lemon zest

¼ teaspoon kosher salt

¼ teaspoon ground cinnamon

1. To make the topping, stir together the flour, brown sugar, cinnamon, and salt in a bowl. Scatter the butter over the top. Using a pastry cutter, two knives, or your fingertips, cut in the butter until it is in small pieces. (Alternatively, pulse the topping ingredients in a food processor until the butter is in small pieces.) Stir in the pecans.

2. To make the filling, toss the berries with the sugar, lemon zest, salt, and cinnamon in a small bowl. Set aside.

3. Preheat the oven to 350°F, with a rack in the lower third. Butter a 9-inch square baking pan.

4. To make the cake, stir together the flour, baking powder, and salt in a small bowl. Set aside.

5. In the bowl of a standing mixer fitted with the paddle attachment (or with a handheld mixer), beat together the butter and sugar, first on low speed and then increasing to medium speed as the ingredients come together, until light and creamy, about 5 minutes. Mix in the egg and vanilla. Stop and scrape down the bowl as needed. On low speed, add half of the flour mixture, then all of the milk, and then the remaining flour mixture, beating just until combined after each addition. Stop to scrape down the bowl after each addition.

1 cup unbleached all-purpose flour

1½ teaspoons baking powder

½ teaspoon kosher salt

½ cup (1 stick) unsalted butter, softened

¾ cup granulated sugar

1 large egg

½ teaspoon pure vanilla extract

½ cup whole milk

Heavy cream, cold; lightly sweetened, softly whipped cream; or ice cream, for serving (optional)

6. Transfer the batter to the prepared pan and smooth the top with a spatula. Scatter the berry filling evenly over the batter. Distribute the topping evenly over the berries, squeezing it in your hands to make some small clumps as you go.

7. Bake until the topping is golden and a toothpick inserted near the center (avoiding the berries) tests clean, 50 to 55 minutes. Let cool on a wire rack for at least 30 minutes before serving.

8. Serve warm or at room temperature, cut into squares. Pass a pitcher of cold cream at the table, or top with whipped cream or ice cream just before serving, if desired.

CRANBERRY-ORANGE OAT BARS

MAKES
24
BARS

These chewy, sweet-tart bars are a perfect picnic dessert or afternoon pick-me-up. In fact, since they are loaded with wholesome oats and antioxidant-packed cranberries, you don't even need to feel guilty about sneaking one for breakfast. If you aren't in a cranberry-growing region, substitute frozen cranberries for the fresh ones (no need to thaw). For the chewiest bars, look for whole dried cranberries.

SEASON TO TASTE: Substitute chopped, fresh and dried cherries, apricots, blueberries, or figs for the cranberries. Or add ½ cup chopped walnuts to the oat crumble.

FILLING

4 cups fresh cranberries

1 cup fresh orange juice

½ cup plus 2 tablespoons granulated sugar

1 cup dried cranberries

2 teaspoons finely grated orange zest

½ teaspoon ground allspice

OAT CRUMBLE

1½ cups unbleached all-purpose flour

1½ cups old-fashioned rolled oats

½ cup firmly packed dark brown sugar

1 teaspoon baking powder

½ teaspoon kosher salt

½ cup (1 stick) unsalted butter, cold, cut into 8 pieces

¼ cup whole milk

1. Preheat the oven to 350°F, with a rack near the center. Butter a 13-by-9-inch baking pan.

2. To make the filling, stir the fresh cranberries, orange juice, and granulated sugar in a saucepan over medium heat until the sugar is completely dissolved. Bring to a boil and cook, stirring occasionally, until most of the berries pop and the juices turn syrupy, about 5 minutes. Stir in the dried cranberries, orange zest, and allspice. Transfer to a wide, shallow bowl to speed cooling and set aside.

3. To make the oat crumble, stir together the flour, oats, brown sugar, baking powder, and salt in a bowl. Scatter the butter over the top. Using a pastry blender or two knives, cut in the butter until it is in pieces just a little bigger than the oat flakes (a few pea-size pieces are fine, too). Stir in the milk just to moisten the dry ingredients.

4. Sprinkle half of the oat crumble evenly in the prepared pan. Using your hands or the bottom of a drinking glass, pack it firmly onto the bottom. Pour the cranberry mixture over the base and spread evenly. Sprinkle the remaining oat crumble evenly over the top, pressing down gently with the palm of your hand to compact.

5. Bake until the top is golden, about 45 minutes. Let cool on a wire rack for at least 1 hour.

6. Cut the sheet lengthwise into 4 equal strips, then cut crosswise into 6 equal strips to make 24 bars. Store the bars in a tightly covered container at room temperature for up to 1 week.

MAKES

9

SERVINGS

This takeoff on the British classic is easier to make than the original and is every bit as delicious. It comes together quickly without heating the oven, so it is perfect for a hot summer day. Cutting the bread into small cubes and mixing it with the berries ensures a balanced distribution of fruit and juice and is less time-consuming than cutting and shaping the bread to the mold. Plan to prepare the dessert 24 hours before serving to compact and infuse the bread with the fruit and its juices.

Use a dense, good-quality white sandwich bread such as *pain de mie*, a sweet (not sourdough) bâtarde, or a brioche loaf. You will need about 12 ounces before trimming the crusts. This is a great use for bread that has gone a bit dry.

SEASON TO TASTE: You can use any combination of berries in this pudding as long as you have plenty of (predominantly red) juice. Red currants are traditional and lend a sweet-tart note. Strawberries should be ripe, juicy, and full of flavor. Ripe peaches, plums, or nectarines, peeled and cut into berry-size pieces, may be substituted for up to one-fourth of the berries.

4 pints (about 8 cups) mixed berries, such as strawberries, raspberries, blackberries, and red currants

⅔ cup granulated sugar

3 tablespoons water

1 tablespoon framboise or cassis (optional)

½ teaspoon finely grated lemon zest

¼ teaspoon kosher salt

1 tablespoon fresh lemon juice

6 cups ½-inch bread cubes cut from good-quality, day-old white bread with crusts removed

Crème fraîche; clotted cream; or lightly sweetened, softly whipped cream, for serving

1. Set aside 1 cup of the mixed berries for garnish. Combine the remaining berries, sugar, water, liqueur (if using), lemon zest, and salt in a large, heavy nonreactive saucepan over medium-low heat. Bring to a gentle simmer, stirring until the sugar is completely dissolved and the berries give up their juices, about 5 minutes. Press down on any large blackberries to crush them slightly and coax out their juices, but leave most of the berries whole. Remove from the heat and stir in the lemon juice.

2. Spoon out 1 or 2 tablespoons of the juices from the cooked berries and mix with the berries set aside for garnish. Cover and refrigerate the berries for garnish until serving time.

3. Using a large spoon, gently stir the bread cubes into the berries in the saucepan until you no longer see any white from the bread. Spoon the mixture into nine 6-ounce ramekins or custard cups, dividing it evenly and pressing down to compact it. Cover the ramekins with plastic film and set on a shallow plate or in a baking pan to catch the

CONTINUED >

juices that will drip out. Weight each ramekin with a can of beans or soup or other weight that fits snugly inside the rim, and refrigerate for 18 to 36 hours, removing the weights after about 18 hours.

4. Remove the plastic film from the ramekins. Slide a knife around the inside edge of a ramekin to loosen the sides of the pudding, then invert a dessert plate on top and invert the ramekin and plate together. Tap the bottom of the ramekin if needed to release the pudding, or give the pudding another nudge with the knife by running it again along the wall of the ramekin to break the seal. Lift off the ramekin. Unmold the remaining puddings the same way.

5. Spoon the reserved berries and juices over and around the puddings, drizzling with additional liqueur, if desired. Pass the crème fraîche at the table.

MAKES

6

SERVINGS

The delicate, graceful, and airy Pavlova originated in Australia as a tribute to Russian ballerina Anna Pavlova. There, it is filled with kiwifruit, passion fruit, and gooseberries. But the beauty of these meringue shells piled high with cream and topped with fresh fruit is their adaptability to any place or season. Here, berries are the star. Mix raspberries, blueberries, and blackberries, or choose whatever berries look best at your market.

Be sure your bowl and beaters are sparkling clean for the best volume when whipping the whites. Vinegar may sound like an unusual addition, but it helps give the snow-white meringue its classic crunchy outside and chewy center.

You can make the meringue shells and lemon-lime curd a day in advance. To retain their shattering, crisp texture, leave the shells in the closed oven and fill them right before serving.

SEASON TO TASTE: Top the meringue shells with any soft fruits cut into bite-size pieces. Peeled and diced peaches, plums, and apricots; chopped cherries; sliced figs; citrus segments released from their membranes (see Farm Journal, page 109); or cut-up tropical fruits (pineapple, banana, guava, mango) will all work.

MERINGUE SHELLS

4 large egg whites, at room temperature

⅛ teaspoon cream of tartar

Pinch of kosher salt

1 cup Baker's Sugar, superfine sugar, or granulated sugar

1 tablespoon distilled white vinegar

LEMON-LIME CURD

4 large egg yolks

½ cup granulated sugar

1 teaspoon finely grated lemon zest

1 teaspoon finely grated lime zest

CONTINUED >

1. Preheat the oven to 225°F, with a rack near the center. Line a rimmed baking sheet with parchment paper. Turn the parchment over and use a pencil to draw six 4-inch circles, spacing them evenly to leave a little space all around them. Turn the paper back over in the pan and oil the paper lightly.

2. To make the shells, in the bowl of a standing mixer fitted with the whisk attachment (or with a handheld mixer), beat together the egg whites, cream of tartar, and salt on medium speed until the whites hold soft peaks. Add the sugar, a tablespoon or two at a time, beating after each addition to incorporate fully and stopping to scrape down the bowl as needed. When all of the sugar has been added, increase the speed to medium-high and continue to beat until the meringue holds firm peaks when you lift the beater, a few minutes longer. It should look smooth and glossy, like marshmallow creme. On low speed, mix in the vinegar.

CONTINUED >

2 tablespoons fresh lemon juice

2 tablespoons fresh lime juice

4 tablespoons (½ stick) unsalted butter, softened

Pinch of kosher salt

1 cup heavy cream, very cold

1½ pints (3 cups) mixed berries

Finely grated lemon zest and/or lime zest, for garnish

3. Using the circles you marked on the parchment as a guide, mound one-sixth of the meringue onto the center of each circle. Use the back of a spoon or a spatula to create nests with broad, raised rims and a dip in the center to hold the cream and fruit. If you like, swirl the meringue around the edges to create an attractive finish. I like to run my finger around the edge in a circular motion to create a decorative rim.

4. Bake until the shells feel completely dry to the touch, about 1 hour. They should remain white. If they threaten to brown, reduce the oven temperature to 175°F to complete the baking. Turn off the oven with the baking sheet inside and the oven door closed. Leave the shells there until they are completely cool, at least 2 hours or up to 1 day.

5. While the shells bake, make the curd. Whisk together the egg yolks, sugar, and lemon and lime zests and juices in a small, heavy non-reactive saucepan. Add the butter and salt, place over medium-low heat and cook, stirring constantly, until the mixture coats the back of a spoon and leaves a trail when you draw your finger across it, 6 to 8 minutes. Reduce the heat if the mixture threatens to boil.

6. Use a spatula to push the curd through a fine-mesh strainer into a bowl (discard the solids). To cool the curd quickly, fill a larger bowl partway with ice water, and nest the bowl of curd inside it, taking care not to slosh water into the curd. Stir occasionally over the ice water until cool, about 10 minutes.

7. Retrieve the bowl from the ice bath, wipe the bottom dry, and cover the curd with plastic film, pressing it directly against the surface. Refrigerate until cold, about 2 hours or up to 4 days.

8. Using a large spatula, carefully transfer the meringue shells to individual serving plates. (It is fine if a few pieces flake off.) Using a chilled bowl and a chilled whisk or beaters, whip the cream until it holds soft peaks. Add the lemon-lime curd and continue whipping until the cream is very thick but still a little soft.

9. Just before serving, pile the cream into the center of the meringue shells, dividing it evenly. Top generously with the berries. Grate a whisper of lemon and/or lime zest over the tops.

A visit to a farmers' market can open up a world of fruit varieties that rarely, if ever, make it onto supermarket shelves. One of my most memorable market discoveries was the Highland pear, grown by Peter and Norma Jensen of Jensen Orchard in Sheboygan, Wisconsin. A cross of the Bartlett and the Comice, the fruit is yellow and lightly russeted when ripe, with sweet, juicy flesh that nearly melts in your mouth. The name comes from a town in New York's Hudson Valley, the area where the hybrid was developed.

When shopping for pears in your local market, choose firm ones for cooking and enjoy the buttery, soft varieties in fruit salads or out of hand. Two of the most commonly available types are the smooth-fleshed, mild-mannered Anjou and the fragrant and flavorful Bartlett, perhaps the prototype pear. The crunchy Bosc is perfect for poaching, holding its elegant, elongated shape well. The Rubenesque Comice is equally beautiful, with sweet, juicy flesh that can do a convincing impression of a peach, running juice down the chin. The Manitowoc market where I met the Jensens was the last I saw of the Highland pear, and I never had a chance to try it in a recipe, but I am sure it would do nicely in place of the Comice.

Other pomes, or fruits with an edible fleshy layer surrounding a tough central core, include apples and quinces. As with pears, you are likely to find a much larger assortment of apple varieties at your farmers' market than at your grocery store, making the market the best—and sometimes only—way to explore what grows in your region. One time, during an emergency after-hours stop at the supermarket in search of apples for a crisp, I was disheartened to find the bins stocked with Red Delicious apples shipped from across the country and

The Meads have been growing fruits and vegetables on 180 acres of farmland in New York's Dutchess County since 1916. Mead Orchards cultivates nearly forty varieties of apples, including Braeburn, Cameo, Cortland, Fortune, Fuji, Gala, Golden Delicious, Idared, Jonagold, Macoun, McIntosh, Mutsu, Northern Spy, Red Delicious (much better than the store variety!), Rome, Senshu, Shizuka, Stayman Winesap, and others. Also at Mead are pears, stone fruits, berries, and winter squashes and pumpkins just waiting to be baked into pies. Three generations of Meads have attended Cornell University College of Agriculture to keep up to date on farming practices and innovations. The Meads take their produce to seven farmers' markets each week, venturing as far south as New York City, and welcome visitors to pick fruit at the farm, where Beth Mead makes you feel right at home as you take in sweeping views of the Catskill Mountains.

Braeburns from Australia, despite it being the height of apple season in a prime apple-growing area.

When selecting apples to use in desserts, choose varieties with dense flesh when you want them to retain their shape, such as for baked apples, and juicier types when you want them to fall apart, such as for applesauce.

If you have never encountered a quince, you may find the rock-hard fruit intimidating. This apple and pear relative comes from a deciduous tree native to southwest Asia. Generally available September through November, the pear-shaped fruit is highly astringent, has dry flesh, and is thoroughly unpleasant when raw. Ah, but cook it and the fruit turns soft and fragrant, with an unmistakable floral flavor. Most, though not all, quince varieties turn a lovely shade of rose when cooked.

Autumn promises not only pome fruits, but also persimmons, dates, and figs. Two main varieties of persimmon are available: the flat Fuyu, which remains crunchy when ripe, and the bell-shaped Hachiya, which is puckery until it turns melting soft like a water balloon, at which point its soft, slippery flesh is sugar-sweet.

The plump, slightly wrinkled fresh Medjool, which many consider the finest date, is grown in Southern California and Arizona and can be found year-round at some farmers' markets in those states. But other varieties available in late summer and early fall, with flesh that runs from dry to moist and delicate to robust, are also good. Fresh dates are easiest to find during the autumn observance of Ramadan, when red Huluwas and yellow Barhis, sold still clinging to the branch, provide the initial burst of energy for many Muslims as they break their daily fast. Dried dates are available year-round, including the sweet, dark Medjool; light amber, firm Deglet Noor; soft, golden Halawi; caramel sweet, soft Khadrawy; and dry Thoory.

Figs have two seasons. The tree typically bears what is known as the breba crop in spring on branches from the previous season, with fruits ripening in July or August. The main crop of figs comes in the fall on the current season's new branches, with fruit continuing to ripen into November. Varieties vary in color, with skin ranging from yellow-green to brown to purple-black, and flesh from white to strawberry to amber and speckled with small, edible seeds.

Selecting and Storing Autumn Fruits

APPLES should have smooth skins and be relatively free of blemishes. Russeting shouldn't be a concern, as it occurs naturally in some varieties. Look to the recipe for guidance on whether you should seek a dense-flesh variety that maintains its shape when cooked, such as the Granny Smith or Braeburn, or a softer type that collapses when cooked, such as the McIntosh. Most often, I seek out apples with a good sweet-tart balance. Especially when caramel is involved, it prevents the dessert from tasting too sweet. Store apples in a vented plastic bag (poke a few holes in it) in the crisper of the refrigerator, usually for a week or two. The staying power of apples depends on the variety, with some keeping for only a week or so and some keeping for much longer. Late-season apples are typically the best keepers. When in doubt, ask the market vendor for advice.

The PEAR is one fruit that is at its best when picked unripe, so there is no need to avoid hard, green pears. To hasten ripening once you have them home, store them in a paper bag or a bowl along with bananas or apples at room temperature until they yield slightly when pressed gently near the stem. Check them daily, as they can go from underripe to overripe quickly. Although it is best to eat pears in the short window after they have reached their peak, you can store ripe pears in a vented plastic bag in the refrigerator crisper for a couple of days, especially if you will be using them in cooking. Refrigerating pears is not optimal, however, as they brown quickly and become mealy. It is better to refrigerate them (in a plastic bag in the crisper) for a few days before they are fully ripe to slow down the ripening process, or to refrigerate hard, green pears for longer. Remove them several days to a week before you need them to allow them to ripen fully. If you are ready to use them and they are not sufficiently ripe, use the paper-bag trick to accelerate ripening.

Large **QUINCES** are the most flavorful. The fruits start out green but ripen to a pale to bright yellow. They remain hard when ripe, so color is your cue for when to start cooking. You can keep them on the countertop when they are green, but once the color begins to change, store them in the refrigerator in the same way you store apples. They should keep nicely for a couple of weeks. Toss them if they become soft or shriveled.

Purchase Fuyu **PERSIMMONS** that are firm and clear of blemishes. Hachiyas, in contrast, should be anywhere from smooth and firm to blackened and drooping. If purchased firm, leave them on a windowsill until they look frighteningly soft, as if the fruit is about to burst through its nearly translucent skin, then scoop out the flesh and refrigerate it in an airtight container for up to 3 days before using.

Fresh **DATES** may be smooth or slightly wrinkled, depending on the variety, and can be eaten at any stage of ripeness, from tart and crunchy to soft and sweet. Ripen fresh dates at room temperature until they darken and soften; they will appear discolored during the transition. Store Medjool dates in an airtight container at room temperature for up to 2 months, in the refrigerator for up to 1 year, or in the freezer for 1 year or longer. Refrigerate other varieties of fresh, ripe dates in an airtight container for 1 to 2 weeks, or freeze for up to 2 months. Store dried dates tightly wrapped at room temperature. Dates sometimes develop a white, powdery film, which is the result of natural sugars crystallizing on the surface. If it bothers you, the folks at Seaview Ranch in Coachella, California, suggest steaming the dates for 10 minutes, or placing them on a baking sheet covered with a damp dish towel and warming them in the oven for a few minutes to melt the sugar crystals.

Look for **FIGS** that are plump and heavy for their size. Because they must be picked fully ripe, figs are fragile and should be consumed soon after purchasing. Take a hint from Marie Simmons, author of *Fig Heaven*: bring empty egg cartons to the farmers' market, nestle each fig in one of the indentations for safe transport home, and leave the original fig basket behind with the vendor to reuse. At home, store figs in a paper bag in the warmest part of the refrigerator for 2 to 3 days.

APPLE, PEAR & QUINCE GALETTE

Quince has a distinctive perfume and taste that you will immediately recognize if you've ever enjoyed the Spanish quince paste called *membrillo*, which is often served with Spain's famed sheep's milk Manchego cheese. This is not a fruit to enjoy raw. But cooked, it transforms to a soft, magnificently fragrant fruit that shows off the personality of its cousins, apples and pears. Take care when peeling and cutting the quince. The hard flesh resists all but the sturdiest knife.

Use a firm, tart apple, such as Granny Smith, Greening, pippin, or Jonagold. For the pears, try Bosc, Bartlett, French Butter, or Comice.

SEASON TO TASTE: If quinces aren't available in your area, substitute an additional apple or pear. Quinces are also delicious in combination with pineapple. This should be no surprise, as one variety is called the Pineapple quince.

CRUST

1⅓ cups unbleached all-purpose flour

½ teaspoon kosher salt

½ cup (1 stick) unsalted butter, cold, cut into 8 pieces

2 ounces cream cheese, cold

About 1½ tablespoons ice water

FILLING

1 large tart apple, peeled and cored

1 large pear, peeled and cored

1 large or 2 small quinces, peeled and cored

2 tablespoons firmly packed light brown sugar

1 tablespoon unbleached all-purpose flour

2 teaspoons fresh lemon juice

1. To make the crust, put the flour and salt in a food processor and pulse a few times to mix. Scatter the butter over the top and pulse until the butter is in pea-size pieces. Break the cream cheese into three or four pieces and add to the food processor. Pulse until the butter and cream cheese are in pieces that vary in size from oat flakes to peas. With the motor running, slowly drizzle in the ice water, a little at a time, adding just enough for the dough to hold together when you pinch a clump between your fingers. Listen for the sound of the motor to deepen, a clue the dough is ready.

2. Transfer the dough to a lightly floured work surface and knead briefly just to bring it together into a ball. Flatten into a disk, wrap in plastic film, and refrigerate for at least 45 minutes or up to 1 day.

3. To make the filling, cut the apple and pear into roughly ½-inch cubes. Coarsely grate the quince on the large holes of a box grater. Put all the fruits into a bowl, sprinkle with the brown sugar, flour, lemon juice, vanilla, and salt, and toss to coat evenly. Mix the butter evenly into the fruit.

4. Preheat the oven to 375°F, with a rack in the lower third. Turn a 17-by-12-inch rimmed baking sheet upside down, and cover the bottom with a sheet of parchment paper.

½ teaspoon pure vanilla extract

Pinch of kosher salt

2 tablespoons unsalted butter, cold,
   cut into small pieces

FINISHES

About 1 tablespoon half-and-half

2 tablespoons turbinado, Demerara, or
   other coarse sugar

⅓ cup apricot preserves

1 tablespoon Calvados, pear brandy, or
   brandy (optional)

5. Place the dough disk between two sheets of lightly floured plastic film and roll out into a 14-inch circle. Peel off the top sheet of plastic film. If the circle is uneven, trim the edge of the dough with a pizza wheel or kitchen shears. Then, using the bottom sheet, flip the dough circle onto the parchment. (It will drape over the edges of the pan.) Carefully peel off the second sheet of plastic film.

6. Arrange the filling evenly over the dough, leaving a 2-inch border around the edges. Using the parchment as an aid, fold the border up and over the fruit, tucking and pleating the pastry to snugly fit over the fruit as you go.

7. To finish, brush the pastry rim with half-and-half and sprinkle the turbinado sugar evenly over the pastry and the filling.

8. Bake until the fruit is tender when pierced with a knife and the dough is golden, about 50 minutes. Let the galette cool on the pan for 15 minutes, then slide the parchment with the galette onto a wire rack to finish cooling.

9. Melt the apricot preserves in a small saucepan over medium-low heat. Stir in the liqueur (if using), then pass through a fine-mesh strainer into a small bowl. Brush the glaze over the warm fruit.

10. Serve the galette warm or at room temperature, cut into wedges.

11. Refrigerate leftover galette, tightly covered, for up to 3 days. Heat on a baking sheet in a preheated 375°F oven for about 10 minutes to crisp the crust before serving.

∾ FARM JOURNAL ∾

Warwick Valley Winery & Distillery, New York state's first microdistillery, ferments ripe, seasonal fruits into ports, brandies, and *eaux-de-vie* with bright fruit flavors, such as Bartlett pear liqueur, Bourbon barrel–aged apple liqueur, and sour cherry and black currant cordials. Pop open a bottle for making the tart's finishing glaze, and then serve the brandy as the perfect accompaniment to the tart. At the winery in season, you can even pick your own apples and pears.

INDIVIDUAL APPLE-PEAR CRISPS

MAKES

8-10

SERVINGS

Making crisps in individual serving dishes guarantees that everyone gets his or her fair share of topping. I use tart Granny Smith apples and crisp Bosc pears; both soften without turning mushy. Golden Delicious, Cortland, Jonagold, or Fuji apples and Bartlett or French Butter pears also work well. I prefer the rustic texture (and nutritional boost) of unpeeled fruit, but feel free to remove the skin if you prefer.

Brandied cream is a perfect complement to the crisp. A scoop of vanilla ice cream or a pitcher of heavy cream passed at the table are great alternatives.

SEASON TO TASTE: Vary the filling by using all apples or all pears, by substituting quinces for some of the fruit, or by tossing in a few handfuls of fresh or dried cranberries. Or, try the crisp in summer with stone fruits, such as peaches or nectarines. Add chopped pecans or walnuts to the topping, if you like.

FILLING

2 pounds tart apples (about 6 medium), cored and cut into ½-inch pieces

2 pounds firm-ripe pears (about 6 medium), cored and cut into ½-inch pieces

⅓ cup firmly packed light or dark brown sugar

2 tablespoons unbleached all-purpose flour

½ teaspoon ground cinnamon

¼ teaspoon kosher salt

¼ cup pure maple syrup

1 tablespoon brandy or fresh lemon juice

1. Preheat the oven to 450°F, with a rack in the lower center. Generously butter eight or ten 6- to 8-ounce ramekins or other individual baking dishes and arrange on a rimmed baking sheet. (If you have a silicone baking mat, line the baking sheet with it to prevent the dishes from sliding.)

2. To make the filling, put the apples and pears in a large bowl. Sprinkle with the brown sugar, flour, cinnamon, and salt and toss to coat the fruit evenly. Add the maple syrup and brandy and stir to mix. Divide the filling evenly among the prepared ramekins.

3. To make the topping, stir together the flour, sugar, and salt in a bowl. Scatter the butter over the top. Using a pastry blender, two knives, or your fingertips, cut in the butter until the mixture is the texture of sand. (A few larger clumps are fine.) Sprinkle the topping evenly over the filled ramekins. Do not pack it down.

4. Bake for 15 minutes. Reduce the oven temperature to 350°F, then continue to bake until the topping is golden and the fruit is tender, about 30 minutes longer. Set aside to cool for 10 to 15 minutes while

1¼ cups unbleached all-purpose flour

½ cup granulated sugar

½ teaspoon kosher salt

½ cup (1 stick) unsalted butter, cold, cut into 12 pieces

WHIPPED CREAM

1 cup heavy cream, very cold

2 tablespoons confectioners' sugar

1 to 2 tablespoons brandy (optional)

you prepare the cream.

5. To make the whipped cream, using a chilled bowl and a chilled whisk or beaters, whisk together the cream and sugar until the cream holds soft peaks. Beat in 1 tablespoon of the brandy (if using), then taste and add more sugar or brandy to taste. Continue beating until the cream holds medium-firm peaks.

6. Carefully transfer the hot ramekins to small serving plates. Top each warm crisp with a dollop of the whipped cream. Pass the remaining cream at the table.

∾ FARM JOURNAL ∾

At Weston's Antique Apple Orchard in New Berlin, Wisconsin, Ken Weston is working hard to preserve apple varieties in his sixteen-acre orchard with more than six hundred trees and more than one hundred varieties. Here, you will find possibly the last remaining Rainbow Cherry in Wisconsin, along with the medieval English Sops of Wine, known for its licorice flavor; the Cornish Gilliflower, dating from seventeenth- or eighteenth-century England; and the French Calville Blanc d'Hiver, a spicy apple with the flavor of banana. Other favorites include Cox's Orange Pippin, the Esopus Spitzenburg—said to be a favorite of Thomas Jefferson—and the Golden Russet, one of the oldest varieties still in cultivation. The barn on the property dates to 1901, and the orchard has been operated by the Weston family since 1936.

BAKED APPLE DUMPLINGS WITH CINNAMON CARAMEL

MAKES

6

DUMPLINGS

This play on a baked apple comes with everything you might wish for: flaky pastry, warm baked apple, nuts and raisins, and a rich cinnamon-scented caramel sauce that oozes out when you cut into the dumpling. If all of that is not enough, serve only half of a dumpling, with a scoop of vanilla ice cream in the cavity and caramel drizzled over the top.

These require some advance planning—the pastry needs 30 minutes to chill (a fine time to make the caramel), and the dumplings, once filled and wrapped, need 1 hour to chill and another to bake. The dumplings can be made up to a day before they are baked, wrapped in plastic film, and refrigerated.

SEASON TO TASTE: Use pears or peaches in place of the apples.

PASTRY

3 cups unbleached all-purpose flour

2 tablespoons granulated sugar

1 teaspoon kosher salt

1 cup (2 sticks) unsalted butter, cold, cut into 16 pieces

4 ounces cream cheese, cold

About 2 tablespoons ice water

CINNAMON CARAMEL

1½ cups granulated sugar

¼ cup light corn syrup

¼ cup apple cider (unfiltered apple juice)

¾ cup heavy cream, at room temperature

½ teaspoon pure vanilla extract

¼ teaspoon ground cinnamon

CONTINUED >

1. To make the pastry, put the flour, sugar, and salt in a food processor and pulse a few times to mix. Scatter the butter over the top and pulse several times until the butter is in pea-size pieces. Break the cream cheese into five or six pieces and add to the food processor. Pulse a few times until the cream cheese is in small pieces. With the motor running, slowly drizzle in 1 tablespoon of the ice water. Then continue adding the ice water, about 1 teaspoon at a time, just until the mixture begins to clump up around the blade. Listen for the sound of the motor to deepen, a clue the dough is ready.

2. Transfer the dough to a lightly floured work surface, gather it into a ball, divide the ball in half, and flatten each half into a rectangle about 7 by 5 inches. Wrap separately in plastic film and refrigerate for at least 30 minutes or up to 1 day. (If longer than 45 minutes, remove from refrigerator 15 minutes before rolling.)

3. To make the caramel, stir together the granulated sugar, corn syrup, and cider in a 2½-quart saucepan over medium heat, until the sugar is completely dissolved. Reduce the heat to low, cover, and simmer for 3 minutes. Remove the cover, raise the heat to medium, bring to a boil, and continue cooking without stirring (swirl the pan as needed for even cooking) until the caramel turns a deep amber, about 10 minutes longer.

CONTINUED >

¼ teaspoon sea salt, such as gray salt, fleur de sel, or Maldon sea salt

6 small apples, 2 to 2½ inches in diameter

¼ cup raisins

¼ cup walnuts, toasted and chopped medium-fine

2 tablespoons turbinado, Demerara, or other coarse sugar

¼ teaspoon ground cinnamon

1 large egg white, lightly beaten with 1 teaspoon water

4. Remove from the heat and, standing back to avoid spatters that can burn, carefully pour in the cream. The caramel will bubble furiously. When the fury subsides, return the pan to medium heat and stir with a wooden spoon to form a smooth caramel, about 3 minutes. Remove from the heat and stir in the vanilla, cinnamon, and salt. Set aside.

5. Place one pastry rectangle between two sheets of lightly floured plastic film and roll into a 21-by-7-inch rectangle. Roll lengthwise from the center to the edges, alternating one direction and then the other and avoiding rolling over the ends. (With patience, it will reach the correct size. If the dough softens too much to continue, refrigerate for 10 to 15 minutes and try again.)

6. Peel off the top sheet of plastic film and cut the pastry crosswise to form three 7-inch squares. Cover with a new sheet of plastic film and slide the pastry, still between the sheets, onto a rimless baking sheet and refrigerate. (Unless your baking sheet is very large, the pastry will drape off the end.) Repeat with second pastry rectangle and refrigerate until needed.

7. Cut a thin slice from the bottom of each apple so it stands upright. Using a vegetable peeler or paring knife, remove the peel from the top and bottom of each apple, leaving about a 2-inch band of skin in the middle. Working from the stem end, and using a melon baller or apple corer, cut out the core from each apple, making a generous cavity and leaving about ¼ inch of flesh intact at the bottom to hold the filling. Stir the raisins and walnuts together in a small bowl.

8. Using the first set of chilled pastry squares, center one apple on each of the three squares. Fill the cavities loosely with half of the raisin-walnut mixture. (You may not need it all.) If the caramel has thickened, warm it over low heat, then spoon the caramel over the nuts and raisins in each cavity, allowing it to drip down between them, until the cavity fills. Set aside the remaining caramel.

9. Starting with one apple, pull up the four corners of the pastry to meet in the center at the top of the apple and pinch or twist the pastry closed. (It's okay to stretch the dough a bit if needed.) Press the flaps of dough firmly against the sides of the apple in a pinwheel fashion, all moving in the same direction, to enclose the apple completely.

(Firming the dough against the apples and at the top is the key to preventing the dough from slipping down as it bakes.) Repeat to enclose the remaining two filled apples, then repeat the filling and wrapping with the second set of pastry squares and the remaining three apples.

10. Place the dumplings on a rimmed baking sheet lined with parchment paper or a silicone baking mat. Refrigerate for at least 1 hour or up to 1 day. Refrigerate any remaining caramel in a covered container.

11. Preheat the oven to 425°F, with a rack in the lower third.

12. Mix together the turbinado sugar and cinnamon in a small bowl. Brush the dumplings with the egg white and sprinkle the cinnamon sugar evenly over them. Bake for 10 minutes, then reduce the oven temperature heat to 325°F and continue baking until the pastry is brown, about 50 minutes longer, rotating the sheet front to back about halfway through baking. Let cool for at least 15 minutes before serving.

13. Warm the reserved caramel and drizzle on individual serving plates, then top with a dumpling.

∾ FARM JOURNAL ∾

Look for apple varieties that soften well but do not fall apart in the oven. Granny Smith, Gravenstein, pippin, Golden Delicious, Cortland, Empire, and Jonagold apples will all work well. Small apples are easiest to wrap in pastry. The apple growers at your market will know their varieties best.

MAKES

6–8

SERVINGS

Face it: when you get to the end of the caramel on a caramel apple, the fun is over. This recipe ensures you won't bite off the outer layer and toss the rest of the apple. I like to dip half of the apples in caramel only for the purists, and dip the rest in a combination of caramel and melted chocolate and then coat them with chopped toasted nuts. If you are a fiend for salted caramel—and aren't using the salted nuts—grind or sprinkle a bit of gray salt or *fleur de sel* over the dipped apples while the caramel is still warm.

Be sure the apples are completely dry and at room temperature to ensure the caramel will adhere. If you think the apples may be waxed, scrub them well under hot water and dry thoroughly. If you can't find lollipop sticks, look for plastic stir sticks, or cut wooden skewers into roughly 4-inch lengths with sharp kitchen shears, pulling off any wood that splinters.

SEASON TO TASTE: Pears and caramel are another great combination. Look for the diminutive, sweet Seckel pear or other varieties of small European or Asian apple pears. You can use larger apples or pears, but you won't be able to coat as many.

Twelve 4-inch squares of waxed paper

Vegetable oil pan spray

12 lollipop sticks

12 crisp, tart apples, about 2 inches in diameter

SALTED CARAMEL

1½ cups granulated sugar

¼ cup apple cider (unfiltered apple juice)

2 tablespoons light corn syrup

2 tablespoons dark corn syrup, or 1 additional tablespoon light corn syrup and 1 tablespoon unsulfured dark molasses

1. Arrange the waxed paper squares on a rimmed baking sheet and coat them with pan spray. Insert a lollipop stick into the top (stem end) of each apple.

2. To make the caramel, stir together the sugar, cider, light and dark corn syrups, and cream in a heavy 2½-quart saucepan over medium-low heat, until the sugar is completely dissolved. Brush down the sides of the pan with a pastry brush dipped into cold water to dissolve any sugar crystals clinging to them, then bring the mixture to a boil. Clip a candy thermometer to the side of the pan and boil without stirring (swirl the pan as needed for even cooking), reducing the heat as needed to make sure the caramel doesn't boil over, until the caramel reaches 242° to 245°F, about 10 minutes. (To test without a thermometer, dribble a little caramel into a small glass of ice water. If it forms a firm ball that flattens when pressed between your fingertips, it is ready.)

3. Immediately remove the pan from the heat and stir in the vanilla and salt. Stir occasionally off the heat until the caramel is 230°F, or until it thickens enough to coat the apples without quickly running off.

¾ cup heavy cream, at room
 temperature

½ teaspoon pure vanilla extract

¼ teaspoon sea salt, such as gray salt,
 fleur de sel, or Maldon sea salt

OPTIONAL TOPPINGS

½ cup walnuts, pecans, peanuts, or
 pistachios, toasted and chopped
 medium-fine

Small pinch of sea salt or kosher salt

4 ounces bittersweet chocolate (60 to
 70 percent cacao)

4. Working quickly once the caramel texture is just right, swirl an apple in the caramel, using a spoon to help coat the top and sides. Draw the bottom of the apple across the edge of the pan to remove any excess caramel. Hold the apple upside down for a moment to let the caramel drip toward the top, then turn back over to place the apple on a waxed-paper square. Repeat with the remaining apples. Leave at room temperature until set, at least 1 hour or up to 2 days, draping plastic film over them after they are set.

5. To prepare the optional toppings, put the nuts in a small bowl and mix in the salt. Melt the chocolate in the top of a double boiler over (but not touching) gently simmering water, stirring until it is completely melted and perfectly smooth. (Or, melt in a microwave oven.)

6. Remove an apple from its paper square and dip the bottom third into the warm melted chocolate. Press nuts onto the chocolate around the sides (not on the bottom), and return the apple to its paper square. Repeat until you have coated as many apples as you like with the chocolate and nuts. Leave at room temperature until set, at least 30 minutes or up to 2 days, again draping plastic film over them after they are set.

7. Serve the apples on plates with forks and knives, or with plenty of napkins to enjoy kid-style.

∿ FARM JOURNAL ∽

The small apples that are often more difficult for a farmer to sell are perfect for this recipe. Look for crisp, tart varieties. Windrose Farm in Paso Robles, California, helped me to select their spicy Smokehouse apples, originally grown in Lancaster County, Pennsylvania; Ashmead's Kernel, a russeted apple with deep flavor and a dense texture; and tiny Red Vein crabapples. Each delighted with its own charms. Granny Smith and Empire apples are sure bets. The latter is a cross of Red Delicious and McIntosh, with crisp flesh and a more complex sweet-tart flavor than either of its parents.

GINGER-PEAR SKILLET CAKE

MAKES

8–10

SERVINGS

Moist and spicy, this cake is baked and served in a cast-iron skillet for great taste and a home-spun look. With the fruit on top, there is no need to unmold it. Cloves are a love-it or hate-it kind of spice, so omit them if you are on the hate-it side. Use a flavorful pear variety that will hold its shape reasonably well when cooked. Bosc, Anjou, or French Butter work well.

The cake is delicious the day it is made, but I like it even better the next day, when the flavors have deepened and the texture goes from cakey-tender to a bit more dense. It will stay moist for several days after that, and also freezes well.

SEASON TO TASTE: Try apples or apricots in place of the pears. Or, eliminate the topping and serve the cake with a fresh-fruit compote.

CAKE

2⅓ cups unbleached all-purpose flour

1½ teaspoons ground ginger

1 teaspoon kosher salt

1 teaspoon ground cinnamon

½ teaspoon ground allspice

¼ teaspoon ground cloves (optional)

¾ cup canola, grapeseed, or other neutral vegetable oil

½ cup gently packed light brown sugar

½ cup unsulfured dark molasses

½ cup plain whole-milk yogurt or sour cream

1 tablespoon finely grated fresh ginger

1 large egg, at room temperature

1 teaspoon baking soda

½ cup hot, freshly brewed strong coffee or boiling water

CONTINUED >

1. Preheat the oven to 325°F, with a rack in the lower third. Oil a 10- or 11-inch cast-iron skillet.

2. To make the cake, stir together the flour, ground ginger, salt, cinnamon, allspice, and cloves (if using) in a bowl. Set aside.

3. Whisk together the oil, brown sugar, molasses, yogurt, fresh ginger, and egg in a large bowl until well blended and smooth. Using a wooden spoon or spatula, stir in half of the flour mixture. Stir the baking soda into the hot coffee until dissolved, then add to the batter and stir until combined. Stir in the remaining flour. Transfer the batter to the prepared skillet and spread evenly.

4. To make the topping, cut the pears lengthwise into ½-inch-thick slices. Arrange the longer slices on the batter in a circle at the edge of the pan, overlapping them slightly and with the narrow ends pointing toward the center. Arrange the shortest slices in a second circle in the center to cover the batter completely. Dot the pear slices with the butter along the outer circle only. Mix together the brown sugar and salt and sprinkle evenly over the top.

5. Bake until the top springs back when you press it lightly in the center and a toothpick inserted in the center tests clean, about 1 hour. Transfer the skillet to the stove top to cool for at least 20 minutes.

CONTINUED >

TOPPING

4 firm-ripe pears (about 2 pounds), peeled and cored

1 tablespoon unsalted butter, cut into small pieces

¼ cup gently packed light brown sugar

¼ teaspoon kosher salt

Tangy Whipped Cream (page 27), for serving (optional)

6. Serve warm or at room temperature, cut into wedges and topped with whipped cream. Refrigerate leftover cake, tightly covered, for up to 4 days, or freeze, tightly wrapped, for up to 2 months. Bring to room temperature before serving.

MAKES

4-8

SERVINGS

Showcase the best pears of the market in this easy dessert. Bartletts work especially well because they have great flavor and soften nicely in the oven but still hold their shape. I prefer leaving the skin on, but if you don't, peel them.

Look for small, crunchy amaretti—rather than the chewy ones—in upscale groceries or Italian markets. Or, substitute other crunchy almond cookies, or even gingersnaps.

SEASON TO TASTE: In summer or early fall, this recipe is perfect with peaches or nectarines. They won't take quite so long to soften, so start checking them about 10 minutes after you fill and return them to the oven.

4 firm-ripe pears, halved lengthwise

2 tablespoons plus 1 teaspoon unsalted butter, softened

4 tablespoons firmly packed light brown sugar

1 teaspoon fresh lemon juice

20 small amaretti (about 2½ ounces total weight)

Pinch of kosher salt

Premium vanilla ice cream, or 1 cup mascarpone or whipped cream flavored with 1 to 2 teaspoons amaretto liqueur, for serving

1. Preheat the oven to 375°F, with a rack near the center. Use a melon baller to core the pears, making a small, round cavity in each half.

2. Put the 2 tablespoons butter into a baking pan just large enough to hold all the pear halves in a single layer without crowding. (Don't put the pears in the pan yet.) Sprinkle 3 tablespoons of the brown sugar and the lemon juice over the butter. Place in the preheating oven until the butter is melted and bubbly, about 5 minutes.

3. Stir the melted butter and sugar with a flat whisk to combine (don't worry if it remains somewhat separated). Arrange the pear halves, cut-side down, in the pan and bake until they begin to soften, 15 to 20 minutes.

4. While the pears bake, put the cookies in a plastic bag and crush with the bottom of a heavy skillet or a rolling pin to make medium-fine, uneven crumbs. Pour the crumbs into a bowl and stir in the salt and the remaining 1 tablespoon brown sugar. Using your fingertips, rub in the remaining 1 teaspoon butter to coat the crumbs lightly. (Alternatively, combine the cookies, salt, and sugar in a food processor and pulse a few times until reduced to medium-fine crumbs, then pulse in the butter just until combined.)

CONTINUED >

5. Turn the partially cooked pears cut-side up, and brush or spoon some of the caramel from the pan over them (avoid pooling in the cavities). Loosely fill the cavities with the crumb mixture, sprinkling some of it over the flat surfaces of the pears as well.

6. Return to the oven and bake until the pears are completely tender when pierced with a paring knife, 25 to 30 minutes, depending on the type and ripeness of the pears. Set aside to cool slightly, about 10 minutes.

7. Arrange one or two warm pear halves each in shallow serving bowls, and top with a scoop of ice cream or a generous dollop of amaretto-flavored mascarpone. Spoon some of the caramel from the pan over the top and serve.

GRILLED-FIG SUNDAES WITH BALSAMIC "FUDGE"

MAKES

4

SERVINGS

Balsamic vinegar is transformed into a fudgy sauce for this sundae that brings savory flavors over to the sweet side. Use a good-quality balsamic for the sauce: you should enjoy its taste, even though it may be difficult to imagine how it can make such an intensely flavorful dessert sauce. Fini, Giusti, and Lucini are good brands. If a local producer brings balsamic vinegar to your farmers' market, ask for a sample, and if it's tasty, try it!

If you have some extra *vecchio* (twenty-five-year-old or older) *aceto balsamico tradizionale* on hand, you can save a step by substituting it for the balsamic fudge. This traditional balsamic of Modena, Italy, is made by cooking grape must, then aging it in a series of casks of various woods in accordance with strict quality controls. It is an undeniable splurge at one hundred dollars and up for a small bottle.

For the wine in the balsamic fudge sauce, use either a sweet wine, such as port, Maury, Banyuls, or black muscat, or a young, fruity table wine without much oak or tannin, such as a Zinfandel, Grenache, or Merlot.

SEASON TO TASTE: If figs aren't available, substitute peaches or plums, pitted and halved (quartered if large). Thread two parallel rosemary sprigs through each piece for easy turning on the grill.

SAUCE

⅓ cup balsamic vinegar

3 tablespoons sweet or dry red wine

1 to 2 tablespoons granulated sugar

FIGS

8 branches fresh rosemary, about 6 inches long

16 to 20 small to medium fresh figs

Extra virgin olive oil, for brushing

Best-quality sea salt, such as gray salt or fleur de sel

Freshly ground black pepper

1 pint premium vanilla ice cream

1. To make the sauce, combine the vinegar, wine, and sugar (1 table-spoon if you are using a sweet wine, or 2 tablespoons if using a dry wine) in a small nonreactive saucepan over medium heat, stirring until the sugar is completely dissolved. Reduce the heat to a bare simmer and cook, stirring occasionally, until the sauce is thick and reduced by about half, 12 to 15 minutes. Set aside to cool (the sauce will thicken as it cools).

2. Heat a gas, charcoal, or stove-top grill to medium heat.

3. To prepare the figs, pinch your fingers near one end of a rosemary branch and, leaving a small tuft of needles at the top of the branch, pull down along the branch toward the opposite end to remove the needles. Repeat with remaining branches.

CONTINUED >

4. Soak the stripped branches in water to cover for at least 20 minutes to help prevent them from catching fire on the grill. Chop enough of the removed rosemary needles medium-fine to yield about 4 teaspoons, and set aside to use as a garnish (reserve any remaining needles for another use).

5. When the grill is hot and the branches are well soaked, trim the stems from the figs, cut the figs in half through the stem end, and line up five small or four larger fig halves, cut-side down, on a flat surface. Thread a rosemary branch through the backs of the figs to secure them on the branch. Brush the figs lightly with olive oil on all sides, and sprinkle the cut sides very lightly with salt and pepper.

6. Grill the figs, turning once or twice, until they are warm, soft, and beginning to brown in spots, 6 to 8 minutes.

7. Scoop the ice cream into four bowls. Drizzle the cooled sauce over the ice cream, and sprinkle lightly with sea salt. Crisscross two fig skewers over each bowl and sprinkle with the chopped rosemary. Invite guests to push the figs from the skewers over the ice cream. If you have not used all the sauce, serve the remainder in a small pitcher at the table.

∾ FARM JOURNAL ∽

Look for the best local figs you can find. The small Black Mission, just beginning to wrinkle, is especially sweet. Brown Turkey and Black Jack figs tend to be large, so you will want to use fewer. For white figs, look for Calimyrna or Kadota. If you can find them, the lovely and flavorful Desert King has speckled green skin and a beautiful rose interior.

FRESH FIG BARS

MAKES

30

BARS

The fig bars you find on grocery-store shelves or in the bins at health food stores are made with dried figs. Fresh figs give this cookie a softer texture and bright fig flavor.

The dough can be made up to 2 days ahead, and the bars can be filled and readied to bake up to a day in advance.

SEASON TO TASTE: Substitute apricots for the figs. Or use dried figs, apricots, peaches, or pears, soaking 2 cups of the dried fruit in 1¼ cups water for an hour to plump them. Use the fruit and any of the unabsorbed liquid in the filling, and allow extra time for the fruits to soften when you cook them.

FILLING

1½ pints (about 3 cups) fresh figs, stemmed and quartered

¼ cup granulated sugar

¼ cup moderately assertive honey, such as buckwheat or wildflower

1 tablespoon brandy or fresh orange juice

¼ teaspoon kosher salt

DOUGH

1¼ cups white whole-wheat flour or whole-wheat pastry flour

¾ cup unbleached all-purpose flour

½ teaspoon baking powder

½ teaspoon kosher salt

4 tablespoons (½ stick) unsalted butter, softened

2 ounces cream cheese, softened

⅓ cup firmly packed dark brown sugar

CONTINUED >

1. To make the filling, combine the figs, sugar, honey, brandy, and salt in a heavy saucepan over medium heat. Simmer, stirring occasionally, until the figs are very soft and the liquid thickens slightly, about 5 minutes.

2. Remove from the heat and puree with an immersion blender or in a food processor until smooth, or nearly so. If the fruit already has a thick, jamlike consistency, the filling is done. If not, return to medium heat and cook, stirring frequently to prevent scorching, until the mixture resembles a thick jam, about 5 minutes longer. Set aside to cool.

3. To make the dough, stir together the whole-wheat flour, all-purpose flour, baking powder, and salt in a small bowl. In the bowl of a standing mixer fitted with the paddle attachment (or with a hand-held mixer), beat together the butter, cream cheese, and brown sugar on medium speed until light and creamy, about 5 minutes. Mix in the eggs, one at a time, beating well and stopping and scraping down the bowl after each addition. Mix in the vanilla. Using a wooden spoon, stir in the flour mixture, about 1 cup at a time, to form a stiff dough.

4. Transfer the dough to a floured work surface, flatten into a rectangle, wrap in plastic film, and refrigerate for at least 1 hour or up to 2 days.

CONTINUED >

2 large eggs

½ teaspoon pure vanilla extract

1 large egg, lightly beaten with
  1 teaspoon water

5. Place the dough rectangle between two sheets of lightly floured parchment paper and roll out into a 15-by-10-inch rectangle, picking the dough up and throwing a little flour underneath, as needed, to keep it from sticking. (With patience it will reach the correct size. If the dough resists, let it rest for 15 minutes and try again.) Carefully peel off the top parchment sheet and neatly trim the edges of the dough.

6. Using a pizza wheel or sharp knife, cut a line down the length of the rectangle to make two long strips each 15 by 5 inches. Without cutting through the dough, mark the dough lengthwise down the center of each strip.

7. Spread half of the filling down the inside half of one strip, filling in the area from the center mark to within ½ inch from the long cut edge, and leaving a ½-inch border at the top and bottom. Spread the other half of the filling down the inside half of the other dough strip in the same fashion. Slide a rimless baking sheet under the parchment for support. If the dough has gotten soft or sticky, refrigerate until firm before proceeding.

8. Using the parchment as an aid, lift and fold the uncovered half of one dough strip over the filling to completely enclose it. If the parchment sticks to the dough, carefully peel it back from the dough so the parchment once again lies flat. Repeat with the second strip of dough. You will have two long, filled strips. Press along the three cut sides with your fingers to tightly seal the top and bottom layers of dough. Carefully shimmy one folded strip away from the other strip so the strips are about 1 inch apart.

9. Refrigerate the strips on the baking sheet for at least 30 minutes or up to 1 day. (Cover with plastic film if leaving for longer than an hour.)

10. Preheat the oven to 350°F, with a rack near the center.

11. Brush the tops of both strips with the egg wash. Using a sharp, heavy knife and cutting straight down, cut the strips crosswise into 1-inch-wide bars, but do not pull them apart.

12. Bake until golden brown, 30 to 35 minutes. Slide the bars and parchment onto a wire rack to cool completely. When cool, break the bars apart where you cut them.

13. Store in an airtight container at room temperature for up to 3 days, refrigerate for up to 1 week, or freeze for up to 1 month (thaw at room temperature).

∾ FARM JOURNAL ∾

Rick and Kristie Knoll are harvesting their ten acres of fig trees from June into November at their biodynamic Tairwá-Knoll Farms in Brentwood, California. Adriatics are first out of the gate in spring, followed by Black Missions and Kadotas. Wrapping up the fall crop are Brown Turkeys around—you guessed it—Turkey Day.

DATES & FIGS with FROMAGE BLANC & TOASTED NUTS

I favor the large, plump, chestnut-colored Medjool date for this recipe. For figs, choose the plumpest, sweetest variety available fresh at your market. The Black Mission is reliably sweet, but try one of the other delicious types you discover at the market. If the figs are very large (the Black Jacks on my tree, similar to Brown Turkeys, are enormous!), you will need only half as many. In this case, you may prefer to cut them in half, scoop out a bit of the inside with a melon baller, and mound the cheese in the center, rather than stuff the whole fruits.

Fromage blanc is a fresh cheese with a slight tang and a texture that varies from whipped cream cheese to thick sour cream. Seek out a fuller-fat (4 percent or more) version for this recipe.

SEASON TO TASTE: Fresh dates are a fall crop, but you can find them dried year-round. Figs are also readily available dried and both work well in this recipe. You can substitute another fresh, mild cheese for the fromage blanc, such as whole-milk ricotta, soft-style farmer cheese, mascarpone, or a mild goat cheese.

FILLING

½ cup fromage blanc or other mild fresh cheese, softened

About 2 teaspoons heavy cream or half-and-half

1 to 2 tablespoons aromatic honey, such as blackberry or thyme, plus more for drizzling

⅛ teaspoon sea salt, such as gray salt or fleur de sel

Pinch of white pepper

¼ cup chopped toasted pistachios

12 fresh figs, preferably a mix of green and black varieties

12 large fresh dates

1. To make the filling, stir together the cheese, cream, 1 tablespoon honey, salt, and pepper in a small bowl until smooth. Taste and add more honey, if desired, and more cream, if needed, to achieve a soft, spreadable texture. Stir in the chopped pistachios.

2. Trim the stems from the figs. Stand one fig on its base and cut straight down through the stem end with a paring knife, stopping about three-fourths of the way through the fig, so the bottom remains intact. Make a second perpendicular cut to divide the fig into quarters, again stopping short of the bottom so the fruit is held together at the base. Repeat with the remaining figs.

3. Cut a lengthwise slit through one side of each date and pull out the pit, leaving the date hinged like an open book.

4. Fill each fig and each date with a heaping teaspoon of the cheese mixture. Gently press the quartered figs together with your fingers so they are bursting with the filling. Similarly, press the dates closed so the filling swells from the top.

Handful of lightly salted, toasted whole pistachios, walnuts, pecans, or almonds

Small, pesticide-free edible whole flowers or flower petals, such as tiny pansies, for garnish (optional)

5. Place the stuffed fruits on a platter. Scatter the whole pistachios around them. Warm some honey slightly by immersing the closed jar in a saucepan of hot water, or by pouring it into a small dish and heating in a microwave oven just until warm enough to be easily pourable, about 10 seconds. Dip a fork or honey dipper into the honey and wave it lightly over the fruits. (This is finger food—be prepared to get sticky!) Scatter the flowers around the platter, if desired, and serve.

∾ FARM JOURNAL ∾

The lion's share of U.S. Medjool dates are grown in California's Coachella and Bard valleys (putting the "palm" in Palm Springs!), along with many other varieties, such as Halawi, Deglet Noor, and Khadrawy. According to the California Medjool Date Council, this variety is unique in that it is sold either fresh or frozen, not dried. Their long shelf life allows Medjools to be enjoyed year-round.

PERSIMMON SWIRL CHEESECAKE IN A GINGERSNAP CRUST

MAKES

12–16

SERVINGS

This cheesecake uses two types of persimmons: the bell-shaped Hachiya that feels like a water balloon about to burst when ripe, and the firm, flat Fuyu. Leftover poaching syrup is delicious mixed with fresh fruit, over crepes or pancakes, or stirred into iced tea or cocktails.

Plan ahead: there isn't much active time, but the cake bakes and rests in the oven for a total of about 2½ hours, and then needs another 12 hours to chill and set.

SEASON TO TASTE: Use pureed cooked pumpkin in place of the persimmon in the filling. Or substitute diced apples or firm-ripe pears for the persimmon in the topping.

CRUST

2 cups (about 6 ounces) crumbled gingersnaps

2 tablespoons firmly packed light or dark brown sugar

4 tablespoons (½ stick) unsalted butter, melted

Pinch of kosher salt

FILLING

3 or 4 very ripe Hachiya persimmons

1½ pounds cream cheese, softened

1¼ cups granulated sugar

¼ cup unbleached all-purpose flour

½ teaspoon kosher salt

5 large eggs, at room temperature

½ cup crème fraîche or sour cream, at room temperature

1 teaspoon gently packed finely grated orange zest

1 teaspoon pure vanilla extract

1. Preheat the oven to 350°F, with a rack just below the center. Line the bottom of a 9-by-3-inch springform pan with parchment paper. Butter the sides of the pan but not the pan bottom or the parchment.

2. To make the crust, put the cookies and sugar in a food processor and pulse until reduced to fine crumbs. Add the butter and salt and pulse just until the crumbs are uniformly moistened. Sprinkle the crumb mixture evenly over the bottom of the prepared pan. Using your hands or the bottom of a drinking glass, pack it firmly onto the bottom and about ½ inch up the sides of the pan. Bake for 10 minutes. Let cool on a wire rack. Raise the oven temperature to 450°F.

3. To make the filling, use a paring knife to carve out the calyx (hard top) from each persimmon (as you would core a tomato). Set a strainer over a small bowl. Use a spoon to scrape the pulp into a blender or food processor, discarding the thin skin and the seed if there is one. Process to break up the pulp, then press the pulp through the strainer. Set aside.

4. In the bowl of a standing mixer fitted with the paddle attachment (or with a handheld mixer), beat the cream cheese and sugar on medium speed until completely free of lumps, about 5 minutes, stopping to scrape down the bowl as needed. On low speed, add the flour and salt until smooth. Mix in the eggs, one at a time, beating just until incorporated and stopping and scraping after each addition. (Mix no more than needed after adding the eggs to avoid adding air.) Mix in the crème fraîche.

1½ cups granulated sugar

1½ cups water

1 vanilla bean, split lengthwise

3 Fuyu persimmons (about 1 pound), peeled and cut into ¼-inch dice

Small piece of lemon peel

¼ teaspoon ground cinnamon

5. Transfer 2½ cups of the filling to a bowl and stir in 1 cup of the persimmon puree and the orange zest. (Reserve any remaining puree for another use.) Stir the vanilla into the remaining (plain) filling. Tap both bowls gently on a firm surface to coax out any bubbles, then prick the bubbles with the tip of a knife.

6. Set the crust-lined pan on a rimmed baking sheet to provide insulation and to catch any drips. Pour the plain filling into the crust, then tap the pan gently on the baking sheet to settle the filling and coax out bubbles. Pour in the persimmon filling in a spiral motion, working from the outside to the center. Drag a dinner knife through both layers of the filling in a figure eight, just once, to marble it.

7. Put the baking sheet topped with the springform pan into the oven and bake for 15 minutes. Reduce the oven to 275°F and bake until the cheesecake is slightly wobbly in the center when you gently shake the pan, about 80 minutes longer. Turn off the oven and leave the cheesecake inside, with the door open, for 1 hour.

8. Transfer the cheesecake pan to a wire rack. Run a thin knife around the inside edge of the pan to loosen the cheesecake sides. Refrigerate for at least 12 hours or up to 2 days. To avoid condensation, cover tightly with plastic film only after completely cold.

9. To make the topping, put the sugar into a saucepan and stir in the water. Scrape in the vanilla bean seeds, then drop in the pod. Stir over medium heat until the sugar is completely dissolved and the mixture comes to a boil. Reduce the heat to a bare simmer, stir in the persimmons and lemon peel, and cook just until the persimmons are tender, 6 to 8 minutes.

10. Remove from the heat and pour through a strainer set out over a bowl. Discard the lemon peel and pull out and save the vanilla bean for another use. Transfer the persimmons to a bowl. Return the syrup to the saucepan and boil for 5 minutes to thicken. Stir in the cinnamon and reserved persimmons and remove from the heat. Let cool to room temperature, then refrigerate, covered, until chilled or up to 4 days.

11. Unclasp and lift the outside ring from the springform pan. Slide the cake with the parchment onto a plate. Cut into wedges with a long, thin, sharp knife, dipping the blade into warm water and wiping it clean between slices. Use a slotted spoon to drape some of the chilled persimmon topping over each slice, then drizzle with the syrup, if desired.

C itrus is the sunshine of winter. Just when the market's fruit supply looks as if it might come to a dead halt, citrus trees send out their fragrant blossoms and refreshing fruits. If you live in a citrus-growing region, you will find common and Meyer lemons, regular and Key limes, oranges in their namesake color and in blood red, cocktail-size grapefruits and enormous pomelos, kumquats enjoyed more for their flavorful peel than for their sour seedy interiors, and a parade of mandarins and tangerines to brighten the winter doldrums.

The terms *mandarin orange* and *tangerine* are often confused, but the latter is actually a subset of the former. Mandarins, which are believed to have originated in China and are named for the orange-clad bureaucrats of the emperors' court, are smaller, flatter, and less acidic than oranges. They are a hugely varied group, with the seedless, easy-peeling types like the satsuma and the clementine the most popular in the United States. The term *tangerine* comes from Tangier, the Moroccan port city through which mandarins are believed to have been introduced to the West. In the United States, the term has evolved to cover the entire mandarin territory, creating uncertainty among shoppers. Growers, however, typically distinguish tangerines

by their darker red-orange skin. Varieties include the Fairchild, Fallglo, Sunburst, Murcott, and others. But don't take my word for it. I am still confused about which varieties are actually tangerines!

Meyer lemons, native to China, are believed to be a lemon-orange cross. Their thin skin and sweet, fragrant flesh—much sweeter than the common Lisbon and Eureka lemons—make them a garden favorite in California, where they flourish. On the other coast, in the Florida Keys, little Key limes were brought to the Americas by Spanish and Portuguese explorers from Southeast Asia in the early sixteenth century. The limes have been commercially cultivated for their flavorful juice in the Florida Keys since the late 1800s. Their most popular use is in their namesake pie, but I like to use the juice to bake bars based on the more common lemon bar.

The pomelo is the largest of the cultivated citrus fruits and is relatively sweet, unlike its offspring, the grapefruit, the product of a pomelo-orange cross. Grapefruits may have either white or pink flesh, though both contain compounds that make them bitter as well as sour, a plus for some consumers and a detractor for others. The large Oroblanco (sometimes written "Oro Blanco") is a pomelo and white grapefruit hybrid, with a satisfying balance of sweetness and acidity, and the small Cocktail grapefruit is a cross between a pomelo and a mandarin, with deep yellow flesh and sweet juice reminiscent of orange juice.

Beyond contributing acidity that keeps sweet desserts from becoming cloying and cut fruits from browning, citrus fruits add vibrant flavor to all manner of frozen desserts, cookies and bars, cakes, puddings, and compotes. After extracting the juice or segmenting the flesh, consider using the rinds to make candied peels—a perfect punctuation mark at the end of the meal or a light dessert in its own right.

Selecting and Storing Citrus Fruits

Citrus fruits are sold year-round in most parts of the country, but the best examples are picked ripe for immediate purchase. In general, look for smooth, shiny, relatively thin skins. Varieties like the satsuma, with its rough, pebbly peel, are exceptions. A tinge of green on the skin is more likely a result of climate than ripeness, as cool nights are needed to set the color, and some can revert to green even after they are fully ripened. Generally, pink grapefruits with the deepest blush on the skin will also have the darkest pink or red flesh. The juiciest citrus fruits will be heavy for their size.

Store citrus fruits at room temperature for a few days, or in the refrigerator for up to 2 weeks.

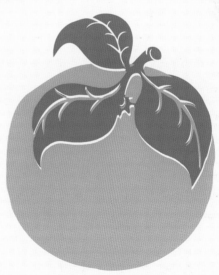

SPICED CITRUS COMPOTE WITH POMEGRANATE SEEDS

MAKES

6

SERVINGS

The syrup for this refreshing citrus compote is infused with the subtle, intriguing flavors of chamomile and spice, using a technique I learned from Deanie Fox, the pastry chef at Ubuntu restaurant in Napa, California. The syrup calls for orange muscat, a sweet wine made from a grape with a naturally orange taste. Quady Winery, in Madera, California, which specializes in dessert wines, bottles an orange muscat labeled Essensia that works nicely in this recipe. Another moderately sweet wine can be used in place of the orange muscat. Or, mix together ½ cup water, ¼ cup fresh orange juice, ¼ cup granulated sugar, and 2 tablespoons orange liqueur such as Cointreau and use in place of the 1 cup wine.

This recipe also calls for pomegranate molasses, or concentrated pomegranate juice, made by reducing pomegranate juice to a thick syrup. You can find the sweet-tart syrup in Middle Eastern markets or in the ethnic-foods section of many supermarkets. It should have only one ingredient: pomegranate juice.

If you remove the peels from the fruits in large strips, you can use them to make Candied Citrus Peels (page 128).

SEASON TO TASTE: Vary the citrus to suit your taste and local availability.

---

1 cup orange muscat wine

¼ cup granulated sugar

Juice and finely grated zest of 1 lemon

2 navel oranges

1 cup kumquats, cut crosswise into thin slices and seeds removed

1 cinnamon stick

6 whole cloves

2 green cardamom pods (optional)

1 chamomile tea bag

1 pink grapefruit

2 blood oranges

4 seedless mandarins, such as satsuma or clementine

1. Stir together the wine, sugar, and lemon juice and zest in a medium nonreactive saucepan. Juice one navel orange and add the juice to the pan along with the kumquats, cinnamon, cloves, and cardamom (if using). Bring to a boil over medium heat, stirring until the sugar is completely dissolved, then reduce the heat to medium-low and simmer, stirring occasionally, for 5 minutes. Remove from the heat.

2. Fully immerse the tea bag in the hot liquid and leave to steep for 4 minutes. Press the tea bag to extract the flavor and remove from the pan, along with the cinnamon stick, cloves, and cardamom pods.

3. Using a paring knife, peel and segment the grapefruit into a bowl as directed in the Farm Journal on the facing page, poking out any seeds as you go. Squeeze the residual juice from the membranes into the bowl. Peel the remaining navel orange and the blood oranges in the same fashion, but rather than segmenting them, cut them into ⅛- to ¼-inch-thick rounds, discarding any white fibers in the center. Add

1 tablespoon pomegranate molasses

About ½ cup pomegranate seeds (see Seeding a Pomegranate, below)

the rounds to the bowl. Peel the mandarins and separate the segments, pulling off any strings that cling to them and poking out any seeds. Add the segments to the bowl.

4. Pour the warm kumquats and syrup over the fruit and stir to combine. Let cool, then cover and refrigerate until chilled, at least 3 hours or up to 3 days.

5. Spoon the fruit and some of the syrup into individual serving dishes. Drizzle ½ teaspoon pomegranate molasses over each serving and sprinkle with pomegranate seeds.

∾ FARM JOURNAL ∾

Follow the advice of Becky Courchesne of Frog Hollow Farm and Bakery in Brentwood, California, on how to peel and section citrus fruits. Cut off both ends of the fruit with a sharp paring knife to reveal the flesh. Stand the fruit on a cut side on a cutting board and cut off the peel from the top to the bottom, following the contour of the fruit and removing all the pith along with it. To release the segments, hold the peeled fruit in one hand over a bowl and cut along both sides of the membrane of each segment, then push the segment out into the bowl.

SEEDING A POMEGRANATE

Put on an apron—pomegranate juice stains! Use a paring knife to cut out the little crown on top as if you were coring a tomato. Score the fruit around the equator, then pull apart with your hands. With your palm over the cut-side, turn the fruit, cut-side down (palm up), over a bowl in the sink and whack the top—hard—with a large, heavy spoon, avoiding your fingers. Many of the seeds will fall out into the bowl. Use your fingers to poke out the resistant seeds. Pull away any membranes that stick to the seeds, or cover the seeds with cool water and skim off the membranes, which will float. The seeds have an edible, fibrous center that is more than compensated for by the brilliant red sac of juice surrounding it.

TANGERINE-SICLE ICE CREAM

This cross between tangerine sorbet and vanilla ice cream will bring you right back to that child-hood favorite, the Creamsicle, but without the stick. If you thought ice cream was only for summer, this refreshing, bright-orange winter treat will change your mind.

SEASON TO TASTE: Use the sweetest, most flavorful mandarins you can find. Satsuma, clementine, or Kishu mandarins or Algerian tangerines are all great choices. Or, substitute fresh orange or blood orange juice.

ICE CREAM

1 cup heavy cream

¾ cup granulated sugar

2 large eggs

½ cup whole milk

¼ teaspoon kosher salt

1½ cups fresh tangerine juice (about 12 tangerines)

2 tablespoons mandarin or plain vodka (optional)

¾ teaspoon pure vanilla extract

TOPPING

4 tangerines

1 teaspoon Baker's Sugar or superfine sugar

Mint sprigs, for garnish

1. To make the ice cream, stir the cream and sugar in a heavy saucepan over medium heat until steam rises from the surface and bubbles begin to form along the edge of the pan.

2. Whisk together the eggs, milk, and salt in a bowl until well combined. Whisking constantly, slowly pour in the hot cream, then return the mixture to the saucepan. Cook over medium-low heat, stirring constantly and scraping the bottom with a wooden spoon, until the mixture thickens enough to coat the back of the spoon, about 6 minutes. Do not let the mixture boil. Pour through a fine-mesh strainer into a bowl.

3. Place the bowl into an ice bath and stir occasionally until almost cool. When it is close to room temperature, remove from the ice bath, stir in the tangerine juice, vodka (if using), and vanilla. Cover and refrigerate for several hours until very cold, or place in the freezer for about 1 hour.

4. Freeze in an ice-cream maker according to the manufacturer's instructions until it is no longer becoming any firmer, about 30 minutes. Quickly pack the ice cream into a chilled quart container and "thunk" the container on the countertop a couple of times to remove air pockets. Press a piece of plastic film or waxed paper directly on top of the ice cream before covering. Freeze until the desired consistency, about 2 hours or up to 1 week.

CONTINUED >

5. To make the topping, finely grate the zest from two of the tangerines and set aside. (A Microplane zester is the ideal tool for this task.) Peel all four tangerines, and remove any visible white pith. Using a sharp paring knife and working over a bowl to catch the juices, hold one tangerine in your hand and cut between the membranes and the segments to release the segments into the bowl. Squeeze the membrane over the bowl to catch the remaining juices. Repeat with the remaining three tangerines. Gently stir in the sugar and reserved zest until the sugar is completely dissolved. Use immediately, or refrigerate in a tightly covered container for up to 1 day.

6. Scoop the ice cream into small bowls and top with the tangerine sections, drizzling a bit of the juices over the ice cream. Garnish with mint sprigs.

HINTS FOR MAKING GREAT ICE CREAM

To make the creamiest ice cream in a home ice-cream maker, be sure to have everything as cold as possible. If using the type with a removable, insulated bowl, put the bowl in the freezer at least 24 hours in advance. I cool the custard base by submerging the lower three-fourths of the bowl in an ice bath (a larger bowl of ice and water), and then slip the setup into the freezer for about an hour so the base gets very cold. (Don't forget it and let it freeze solid.) While the base is chilling, I put the ice-cream maker's beater and cover into the freezer, along with a container for packing the finished ice cream and a spatula.

If your machine allows for it, turn it on and pour the mixture into the machine in a slow stream to begin freezing the custard base quickly. Then process the ice cream a little longer than you think is needed for maximum smoothness and volume. The ice cream is done when it wraps around the beater and is no longer flowing in the canister. A little alcohol in the recipe lowers the freezing temperature, helping to keep the ice cream scoopable. If after packing and freezing the ice cream it becomes too firm to scoop, transfer the container to the refrigerator for 15 to 30 minutes before serving.

MAKES

24

BARS

My complaint with lemon bars is that they are usually too sweet, erasing the fruit's most fundamental charm. These bars have a tender, thin shortbread crust and plenty of tart-sweet lime filling. And they are even better the day after they are baked.

SEASON TO TASTE: Try these with common (Persian) limes. Or, if you can find the aromatic Rangpur lime (a hybrid of lemon and mandarin orange), originally from India but now also grown in Florida, California, and Hawaii, use it for making the bars, which will turn out wonderfully flavorful though not as tart. You can also make the bars with lemons, though not the Meyer, which is too sweet.

SHORTBREAD CRUST

1½ cups unbleached all-purpose flour

⅓ cup confectioners' sugar, plus more for finishing

½ teaspoon finely grated Key lime zest

½ teaspoon kosher salt

½ cup (1 stick) plus 2 tablespoons unsalted butter, cold, cut into 10 pieces

FILLING

1⅔ cups granulated sugar

¼ cup unbleached all-purpose flour

¼ teaspoon kosher salt

5 large eggs, at room temperature

¾ cup fresh Key lime juice (about 20 limes)

1 teaspoon finely grated Key lime zest

¼ cup half-and-half

1. Preheat the oven to 350°F, with a rack in the lower third. Line the bottom and sides of a 13-by-9-inch baking pan with parchment paper or aluminum foil, extending it about 2 inches beyond the pan all around to aid in removing the bars from the pan.

2. To make the crust, stir together the flour, ⅓ cup confectioners' sugar, lime zest, and salt in a bowl. Scatter the butter over the top. Using a pastry blender, two knives, or your fingertips, cut in the butter until the mixture has the appearance of wet, clumpy sand. It should hold together in clumps when you gently press it with your fingers. (Alternatively, combine the flour, confectioners' sugar, zest, and salt in a food processor and pulse to mix, then scatter over the butter and pulse just until the mixture begins to form clumps.)

3. Scatter the mixture evenly in the prepared pan and use your hands to pack it firmly onto the bottom. Bake until lightly golden, about 20 minutes.

4. While the crust bakes, make the filling. Stir together the sugar, flour, and salt in a bowl. Add the eggs and stir until completely smooth. Add the lime juice and zest and the half-and-half and mix slowly but thoroughly to create a smooth mixture without many air bubbles.

5. When the crust is ready, remove from the oven and reduce the oven temperature to 325°F.

6. Pour the filling over the hot crust and return the pan to the oven. Bake until the filling is just set, 20 to 25 minutes. Let cool completely in the pan on a wire rack, then refrigerate for 30 minutes for easiest cutting.

7. Use the extended ends of the paper to lift the large bar from the pan to a cutting board. Using a sharp, heavy knife, and wiping the blade clean with a damp kitchen towel between cuts, cut lengthwise into 4 equal strips, then cut crosswise into 6 equal strips to make 24 bars. Pack the cooled bars between layers of waxed paper in an airtight container and refrigerate for up to 3 days.

8. Serve cold or at room temperature. Sift confectioners' sugar over the bars just before serving.

∾ FARM JOURNAL ∾

Key limes are a pale yellow-green and have lots of tart, flavorful juice for their size—about 16 to the pound. The bushy, thorn-riddled trees make the limes difficult to pick, so they are seldom grown commercially. However, if you live in or near the Florida Keys—or possibly in another citrus-growing region—you may be lucky enough to find the diminutive fruits at your local farmers' market.

A handheld citrus squeezer (see page 21) eases the work of juicing the many small limes. Unlike their larger citrus relatives, you may find it easier to zest the limes after they have been juiced, holding the skin like a thimble over the fingers of one hand and zesting with the other, carefully avoiding the bitter white pith below the surface.

MEYER LEMON PUDDING

I confess that my source for Meyer lemons is not a farmers' market, but instead the unending supply courtesy of my neighbors' trees—on both sides! If you live in a region where growing these juicy, floral fruits is possible, plant a tree (or move next door to one) and you will never find yourself running to the store for last-minute lemons.

SEASON TO TASTE: Try other citrus fruits, such as limes, tangerines, blood oranges, or common (Eureka or Lisbon) lemons.

3 large egg yolks

½ cup granulated sugar

¼ cup firmly packed light brown sugar

3 tablespoons cornstarch

¼ teaspoon kosher salt

2 cups whole milk, cold

1 tablespoon finely grated Meyer lemon zest

½ cup fresh Meyer lemon juice

2 tablespoons unsalted butter, softened

Softly whipped cream, lightly sweetened or flavored to taste with limoncello liqueur, for serving

1. Pour water to a depth of about 1 inch into the bottom of a double boiler and bring to a simmer. Whisk the egg yolks in a small bowl until blended and set aside near the stove.

2. Whisk together the granulated sugar, brown sugar, cornstarch, and salt in the top of the double boiler off the heat. Add enough milk to make a smooth paste, then stir in the rest of the milk. Add the lemon zest.

3. Place the top of the double boiler over (but not touching) the simmering water and heat, stirring occasionally with a flat whisk or silicone spatula, until the pudding thickens and comes to a simmer. Cook at or just below a gentle simmer for 2 minutes, stirring gently but constantly and scraping the bottom of the pan often.

4. Remove the top pan of the double boiler from over the simmering water and, whisking constantly, mix about 1 cup of the hot lemon mixture into the egg yolks. Scrape the contents of the bowl back into the top of the double boiler. Replace the bowl over the simmering water and cook without fully boiling (the pudding may break an occasional bubble), stirring constantly but not vigorously, until the pudding is as thick as sour cream, about 1 minute longer. Remove from the heat and stir in the lemon juice and butter until smooth.

5. Use a spatula to push the pudding through a fine-mesh strainer into a bowl (discard the solids). Fill a larger bowl partway with ice water, and nest the bowl of pudding inside it, taking care not to slosh water into the pudding. Stir occasionally over the ice water until cool, about 10 minutes. (Stirring vigorously after it sets may thin the pudding.)

6. Retrieve the bowl from the ice bath, wipe the bottom dry, and cover the pudding with plastic film, pressing it directly against the surface. (Alternatively, spoon the pudding into individual serving dishes and press plastic film directly against each surface.) Refrigerate until very cold and set, at least 3 hours or up to 2 days.

7. Serve the pudding in small bowls, topped with a dollop of whipped cream.

∾ FARM JOURNAL ᴥ

A hybrid of a lemon and an orange or a mandarin, the Meyer lemon is sweeter and more aromatic than the common Eureka or Lisbon. Still, Meyer lemons can be used in place of lemons in most recipes where the additional acidity is not essential, with just a slight reduction in the amount of any sweetener that is added. The season for the Meyer typically runs from August to March, though in some places the trees are harvested year-round.

MEYER LEMON–GOAT CHEESE SOUFFLÉ CAKES

MAKES

SERVINGS

Goat cheese is balanced by a little crème fraîche in these rich yet light, lemony cakes. Use a fresh, soft, mild goat cheese such as Redwood Hill Farm's plain chèvre or Cypress Grove's goat's milk fromage blanc, both made in Northern California. The cakes have a soufflélike texture when served slightly warm, transforming to a more cheesecakelike texture after a day in the refrigerator.

SEASON TO TASTE: Substitute common (Eureka or Lisbon) lemons for the Meyer lemons if they are not available in your area. In lieu of berries, serve with the raspberry sauce from the Roasted Peach Melba on page 35. Other good choices are a citrus compote or strawberries macerated in a good-quality balsamic vinegar.

1 cup (8 ounces) soft fresh goat cheese

⅓ cup crème fraîche or sour cream

4 large eggs, separated

¼ cup mild-flavored honey, such as acacia, alfalfa, or clover

3 tablespoons unbleached all-purpose flour

Finely grated zest of 2 small Meyer lemons

1 tablespoon fresh Meyer lemon juice

½ teaspoon pure vanilla extract

¼ teaspoon kosher salt

3 tablespoons granulated sugar

Tangy Whipped Cream (page 27) or lightly sweetened, softly whipped cream, for serving

Berries of choice, for garnish

1. Preheat the oven to 350°F, with a rack in the lower third. Butter eight 6-ounce ramekins. Sprinkle with sugar to coat, tapping out any excess. Select a baking pan at least 2 inches deep and large enough to hold the ramekins without crowding. Line the pan with a folded kitchen towel, to prevent the ramekins from sliding, and place the ramekins in the pan, spacing them evenly. Bring a kettle of water to a boil and remove from the heat.

2. Whisk together the goat cheese and crème fraîche in a bowl until smooth. Add the egg yolks, honey, flour, lemon zest and juice, vanilla, and salt and mix until the mixture is uniform and free of lumps.

3. In the bowl of a standing mixer fitted with the whisk attachment (or with a handheld mixer), beat the egg whites on medium speed until they hold soft peaks. Add the sugar in a slow, steady stream, then increase the speed to medium-high and continue to beat until the whites hold firm peaks. Using a large spatula, gently fold the whites into the cheese mixture until only a few small, white streaks remain.

4. Divide the batter evenly among the prepared ramekins, smoothing the tops. Put the pan on the oven rack, and pour the hot water from the kettle into the pan until it reaches about halfway up the sides of the ramekins, taking care not to splash water into the ramekins.

CONTINUED >

5. Bake until the cakes are puffed and appear firm around the edges but still jiggle slightly when you shake a ramekin gently, 20 to 25 minutes. Carefully remove the ramekins from the water bath to a wire rack and let cool. (They will fall as they cool.)

6. Serve barely warm or at room temperature, or refrigerate for up to 3 days and serve chilled. To avoid condensation, cover tightly with plastic film only after completely cold. Just before serving, top each ramekin with a dollop of whipped cream and a few berries.

∾ FARM JOURNAL ∾

Fromage blanc and quark are European-style fresh cheeses used as spreads and in recipes, both sweet and savory. The curd is stirred to create a smooth texture that ranges in consistency from that of Greek-style yogurt to fresh farmer cheese. In France, fromage blanc (also known as *fromage frais*, or "fresh cheese") is often sweetened and served with fruit as a simple dessert. The cheese is made from skimmed milk and is therefore fat free, though some producers add cream to enhance the flavor and texture. Quark is used in Germany (*quark* means "curd" in German) and across eastern Europe in much the same way fromage blanc is used in France. Like the French cheese, cream may be added to produce a cheese that ranges from fat free to full fat.

In the eastern United States, the Vermont Butter & Cheese Company makes a fat-free fromage blanc and a rich quark with 11 percent butterfat.

Cowgirl Creamery and Bellwether Farms, both in Northern California, make fromage blanc, with Cowgirl Creamery using whole milk. Cypress Grove, also in Northern California, makes a goat's milk fromage blanc. Ronnybrook Farm in Ancramdale, New York, makes a slightly tangy cow's milk fromage blanc with skimmed milk, but it is their fresh cultured farmer cheese made from whole milk that I covet for its nutty brown butter flavor that perfectly captures the pure, rich taste of fresh dairy. Doing things the old-fashioned way at Ronnybrook seems to have its rewards. The farm's motto is "Hopelessly out of date, and proud of it." The milk from Ronnybrook still comes with the cream on top.

MAKES

18

CUPCAKES

These moist, airy cupcakes emanate bright orange flavor. The silky buttercream adds a touch of rich decadence. Sifting the flour before measuring and then sifting again with the other dry ingredients keeps the cupcakes light as a cloud. The egg whites will achieve their greatest volume whipped at room temperature in an impeccably clean bowl with clean beaters. Use a good-quality white chocolate, one made with cocoa butter and no added vegetable oils.

If you have only one muffin tin, put the remaining six liners into ramekins or custard cups and set on a rimmed baking sheet, or put sturdy foil or silicone liners directly onto the baking sheet. If you are concerned about consuming partially cooked egg whites, use pasteurized egg whites in the buttercream. Seek out organic oranges, as you will be including the grated zest.

SEASON TO TASTE: Why not tangerines or Meyer lemons?

CUPCAKES

1¾ cups cake flour, sifted before
  measuring

1¼ cups granulated sugar

2 teaspoons baking powder

½ teaspoon kosher salt

1 cup whole milk

½ cup canola oil

¼ cup fresh orange juice

2 teaspoons firmly packed finely grated
  orange zest

1 teaspoon pure vanilla extract

2 large eggs, separated

CONTINUED >

1. Preheat the oven to 350°F, with one rack in the upper third and one rack in the lower third. Line 18 standard muffin cups with paper liners.

2. To make the cupcakes, sift together the flour, 1 cup of the sugar, the baking powder, and salt into a bowl. Whisk in the milk, oil, orange juice and zest, vanilla, and egg yolks until well combined. Set aside.

3. In the bowl of a standing mixer fitted with the whisk attachment (or with a handheld mixer), beat the egg whites on medium speed until they hold soft peaks. Add the remaining 1/4 cup sugar in a slow, steady stream, then increase the speed to medium-high and continue to beat until the whites hold medium-firm peaks. Using a spatula, gently fold the whites into the flour mixture just until combined.

4. Scoop the batter into the prepared liners, filling them about two-thirds full. Bake until the cupcakes are lightly golden, firm to the touch, and a toothpick inserted near the center of a cupcake tests clean, about 20 minutes. Transfer the pan to a wire rack until cool enough to handle, then transfer the cupcakes directly to the rack to cool completely.

CONTINUED >

2½ ounces white chocolate

3 tablespoons fresh orange juice

¾ cup plus 2 tablespoons granulated sugar

4 large egg whites, at room temperature

½ teaspoon kosher salt

1 cup (2 sticks) unsalted butter, softened, cut into 16 pieces

½ teaspoon pure vanilla extract

1 orange, for finishing

HELP! MY BUTTERCREAM LOOKS CURDLED

If your buttercream unravels as you beat in the butter, be patient. It has not curdled, just separated. Persist and it should come back together into a smooth, glossy frosting. If it still looks curdled after all the butter has been added, place the bowl over (but not touching) simmering water in a saucepan for a few seconds to soften the mixture and warm it slightly, then remove from the heat and mix on low speed until cool and smooth. Repeat the warming and mixing if needed. *Phew—crisis averted!*

5. To make the buttercream, melt the white chocolate in the top of a double boiler over (but not touching) gently simmering water, stirring until it is completely melted and perfectly smooth. (Or, melt in a microwave oven.) Let cool until no longer hot to the touch.

6. Combine the orange juice and sugar in a small nonreactive saucepan over medium heat, stirring until the sugar is completely dissolved. Brush down the sides of the pan with a pastry brush dipped into cold water to dissolve any sugar crystals clinging to them, then bring the mixture to a boil. Clip a candy thermometer to the side of the pan and boil without stirring (swirl the pan as needed for even cooking) until the syrup reaches 240°F. (To test without a thermometer, dribble a little syrup into a small glass of ice water. If it forms a soft ball when pressed between your fingertips, it is ready.)

7. While the orange syrup heats, in the bowl of a standing mixer fitted with the whisk attachment (or with a handheld mixer), beat together the egg whites and salt on medium-high speed until they hold medium-firm peaks. Reduce the speed to medium-low and, with the mixer running, slowly drizzle the hot orange syrup into the whites in a thin stream, directing it along the side of the bowl. When all of the syrup has been added, increase to medium-high and continue to whip until the bowl feels cool to the touch, about 10 minutes.

8. Continuing on medium speed, add the butter, one piece at a time, mixing until each piece is completely incorporated before adding the next one and stopping to scrape down the bowl as needed. On low speed, add the white chocolate and vanilla, mixing just until smooth.

9. Using an icing spatula, or a pastry bag fitted with a no. 10 plain round tip or your preferred tip for frosting, generously frost the cooled cupcakes. (You may not need all of the buttercream.) Just before serving, using a Microplane or other fine grater, grate the zest from the orange evenly over the cupcakes.

10. Refrigerate leftover cupcakes, tightly covered, for up to 3 days. Bring to room temperature before serving. Refrigerate leftover buttercream in an airtight container for up to 1 week. To use, bring to room temperature (it will separate again) and beat until smooth.

MAKES
6–8
SERVINGS

Campari and grapefruit is a classic aperitif. Adding mint and freezing the mixture into fluffy mounds yields a supremely refreshing summer dessert or light palate cleanser between courses.

Clear a flat space in your freezer for the pan before you begin. If you are short of space, freeze the granita in ice cube trays until hard, then process in a food processor to break the cubes into icy slivers.

For added elegance, rub the rims of the chilled martini glasses with a cut lime, then dip and twist in coarse sugar to coat the rims before filling with the granita.

¾ cup granulated sugar

2 tablespoons firmly packed coarsely chopped fresh mint leaves, plus 6 to 8 mint sprigs, for garnish

1 tablespoon firmly packed, finely grated grapefruit zest

1 cup water

2 cups fresh pink grapefruit juice (3 to 4 grapefruits)

⅓ cup Campari

12 to 16 pieces candied grapefruit peel (see page 128), for garnish (optional)

1. Stir together the sugar, chopped mint, grapefruit zest, and water in a saucepan. Place over medium heat and bring to a simmer, stirring or swirling the pan until the sugar is completely dissolved. Remove from the heat and let steep for 5 minutes. Stir in the grapefruit juice and Campari.

2. Strain the mixture through a fine-mesh strainer into a 13-by-9-inch glass dish, pressing on the solids to extract all their flavor. (Discard the solids.) Freeze until thickened and slushy, about 1½ hours. Remove the dish from the freezer, scrape the surface and sides of the mixture with a fork to break up any clumps, and return the dish to the freezer. Continue to scrape every 30 to 60 minutes until you have a pile of light, icy slivers, about 3 hours total.

3. Spoon the granita into chilled martini glasses. Crisscross two pieces of candied grapefruit peel (if using) over each serving, and top with a mint sprig. As you complete each glass, refrigerate it until all of the servings are assembled. When they are all ready, serve immediately, as the granita melts quickly.

4. Freeze leftover granita in a tightly covered plastic container for up to 5 days. It will become more compact over time, but the flavor will be just as lively. Fluff with a fork just before serving.

MAKES

2–3

CUPS

DEPENDING ON SIZE
OF FRUITS AND THIN-
NESS OF PEELS

Serve these sweet-tart peels atop the Pink Grapefruit & Campari Granita with Fresh Mint on page 127, as a garnish for ice cream or other desserts, or in a candy dish. They are lovely with the tips dipped into melted bittersweet chocolate and laid out on waxed paper until set. (Temper the chocolate before dipping if you plan to hold the peels longer than a day; see Fruit & Nut Chocolate Bark with Fleur de Sel, page 187.) Or, finely chop the candied peels and add them to cakes, cookies, and other desserts.

This is a great way to use the peels left from making Spiced Citrus Compote with Pomegranate Seeds (page 108). Choose organic fruits to avoid pesticide residue, artificial coloring, or wax on the skins.

SEASON TO TASTE: The listed fruits are only a suggestion. Use the peels of whatever citrus fruits you like best. Two exceptions are lime peels, which tend to become leathery, and very thin Meyer lemon peels, which tend to fall apart. However, if the Meyer lemon peels are relatively thick, they can be used.

1 grapefruit

1 large navel orange

2 Eureka or Lisbon lemons

1½ cups granulated sugar

¾ cup water

Up to 1 cup superfine sugar or
    additional granulated sugar

1. Use a sharp paring knife to cut the tops and bottoms off of each fruit. Score the fruits top to bottom in 1- to 2-inch-wide segments. Poke your thumb under the top of one of the sections to pull off the peel and whatever white pith comes along for the ride. Repeat to remove the peel from all of the fruits.

2. Lay a piece of peel flat on a cutting surface, pith-side up. Holding a thin, sharp knife with the blade parallel to the peel, carefully shave away and discard as much of the pith as possible. (For fruits with little pith, such as Meyer lemons, there's no need to trim.) Cut the peels lengthwise into strips. The width can range from $1/16$ inch for a delicate garnish to $1/4$ inch for candy or for dipping in chocolate.

3. Put the peels into a 3-quart saucepan and add cool water to cover. (Don't worry if the peels float with the first blanching.) Bring the water to a boil, boil for 5 minutes, then drain the peels in a strainer and rinse briefly under cool running water. Repeat the boiling, draining, and rinsing two more times, using fresh water each time. Leave the peels in the strainer after the final blanching.

4. Stir together the granulated sugar and the ¾ cup water in the same saucepan over medium-low heat until the sugar is completely dissolved. Raise the heat to medium-high and boil without stirring for 2 minutes. As the mixture boils, brush down the sides of the pan with a pastry brush dipped into cold water to dissolve any sugar crystals clinging to them.

5. Stir in the peels, coating them completely, and cook at a gentle simmer, stirring occasionally, until they are tender and nearly translucent, about 15 minutes. Remove from the heat, stir gently again to coat with the syrup, cover, and let stand at room temperature for at least 1 hour or up to overnight.

6. At this point, you can either refrigerate the candied peels in the syrup in an airtight container for up to 4 weeks, pulling them out with a fork or tongs as you need them, or you can coat them in sugar and dry them.

7. To coat the peels in sugar, strain the fruit in a strainer set over a bowl until most of the syrup has dripped off, about 1 hour. (You can refrigerate the syrup for flavoring drinks or desserts.) Line a baking sheet with waxed paper, parchment paper, or a silicone baking mat and place a wire rack over the paper. Put ½ cup superfine sugar into a glass baking dish or shallow bowl. Use tongs to lift the peels, a few at a time, from the strainer and add them to the sugar. Use your hands to coat the peels thoroughly. Shake off any excess sugar and transfer the peels to the wire rack. Continue to coat all the peels, adding more sugar as needed.

8. Leave the peels on the rack at room temperature or in an oven with the pilot lit until dry to the touch, several hours to 2 days. The drying time will vary depending on the moisture remaining in the peels and the temperature of the oven or the temperature and humidity of the room. (You can accelerate the drying by putting the baking sheet into a 100°F oven for 30 minutes, then turning off the oven and leaving them inside until dry.) At this point, you can dip the candied peels in chocolate, if you like.

9. Store sugared peels in an airtight container with waxed paper between the layers at room temperature for up to 1 week or in the refrigerator for up to 1 month. Coat with additional sugar before serving, if desired.

MARKET SURPRISES:
VEGETABLES & TROPICAL FRUITS

When it comes to dessert, you probably don't think of the vegetable side of the produce aisle. Think again. Many vegetables, or fruits masquerading as vegetables, have star qualities when it comes to dessert.

Consider the avocado. Actually a fruit, we typically enjoy it in salads. But it would be a shame not to turn its rich flesh into something sweet and creamy, and in some parts of the world, that's exactly what cooks do. Most of us know that carrots have their place in cake and that sometimes zucchini do, too, but why not add beets to chocolate cake to make it extra moist and dark, or stir some naturally sweet fresh corn kernels along with some berries into the batter for a cornmeal cake? And even though rhubarb is typically treated as a fruit, it is actually botanically a vegetable.

Among the most popular fruits, melons are a refreshing treat on their own, and with the addition of a little citrus and mint, they become something special. Cantaloupes and honeydew melons belong to the large plant family known as Cucurbitaceae, which also includes watermelon, cucumber, winter squashes, pumpkins, and loofah, the stuff of bath sponges.

Although you can probably find plenty of different cucurbits at your local farmers' market, you will likely have more difficulty shopping there for tropical fruits, unless you are lucky enough to live in Hawaii. There, the markets are full of pineapples, coconuts, macadamia nuts, and other tempting fruits and nuts, all waiting to be transformed into cakes, cookies, and more.

Selecting and Storing Vegetables and Tropical Fruits

Choose **CORN** with green husks and moist silk, peeking below the silk to avoid ears with signs of black mold. The kernels should line up in tightly packed rows all the way to the tip, or nearly so. Look for slender to medium-size **CARROTS** with smooth skin, and for **BEETS** that are firm, smooth, and unblemished. **ZUCCHINI** should be firm and without soft spots. Refrigerate corn in its husk in the crisper for up to 2 days and use as soon as possible after purchase, before its natural sugars convert to starch. Store beets—with their tops stored separately—and carrots in plastic bags for up to 10 days.

Choose **MELONS** that are firm and heavy for their size. Most varieties will be fragrant at the stem end, though some are difficult to gauge until you cut them open. It's hard to judge a watermelon by its cover, but the market gives you an opportunity to taste the current harvest before you buy. Once home, keep melons at room temperature until they are ripe, then refrigerate and use within a few days.

Ripe **PINEAPPLE** should smell fragrant and have just a little give when you gently squeeze it. The leaves should be fresh and green. Avoid fruits with large soft spots, which means bruised flesh underneath. A pineapple with a winey smell is overripe. Cut up ripe pineapple, refrigerate in a covered container, and use within a few days.

AVOCADOS soften only after they are picked from the tree, so purchase them hard or yielding to gentle pressure, depending on how quickly you plan to use them. Soften on a windowsill or in a fruit basket. Refrigerate as soon as they are yielding and use within a few days.

RHUBARB ranges in color from green to pink or crimson, depending on the variety. The field rhubarb often found at farmers' markets tends to have a more robust flavor than the cultivated rhubarb sold in supermarkets. Lighter-colored stalks tend to be more sour and astringent, so look for bright red ones to use in desserts. They should be firm and crisp, like celery, and not at all wilted. Choose thin to medium stalks without soft spots or blemishes. Remove the leaves, which are toxic, and refrigerate the stalks in a plastic bag in the refrigerator crisper for 3 to 5 days.

~ FARM JOURNAL ~

Melons prefer a long, warm, frost-free growing season, making the South the preferred region for cultivation. California, Texas, Georgia, Arizona, and Florida are the primary states for commercial crops. But melons have been spotted at farmers' markets in many other states, from Oregon, Minnesota, and Illinois to North Carolina and New York. Depending on the location, the earliest melons are harvested in April, with the season peaking in July and August and continuing in some areas nearly through the end of the year.

CORNMEAL CAKE WITH FRESH CORN & BERRIES

MAKES

8

SERVINGS

Fresh corn, cornmeal, olive oil? Doesn't sound much like dessert. But add ripe berries and a little sugar and you will have a captivating cake that is hard to stop eating. Why shouldn't corn play a starring role in a dessert? Fresh from the field, it's as sweet as most fruits—sweeter than many. This moist cake gets a double-corn wallop, with a little crunch from cornmeal and sweet bursts of fresh corn, all balanced by sweet-tart blackberries. The cake is best the day it is made but will remain moist if stored tightly covered at room temperature for up to 3 days.

SEASON TO TASTE: Substitute other berries, or a combination of berries, for the raspberries.

---

1 pint (about 2 cups) blackberries or raspberries

¾ cup corn kernels (from about 1 ear corn)

1 cup plus 2 tablespoons unbleached all-purpose flour

1 cup granulated sugar

½ cup fine or medium stone-ground yellow cornmeal

1 teaspoon baking powder

¼ teaspoon baking soda

½ teaspoon kosher salt

2 large eggs

½ cup buttermilk

⅓ cup extra virgin olive oil

Lightly sweetened, softly whipped cream, for serving (optional)

---

1. Preheat the oven to 350°F, with a rack near the center. Oil an 8-by-2-inch round cake pan. Dust the pan with flour, tapping out the excess.

2. Set aside 1 cup of the berries for garnish. Put the remaining 1 cup berries into a small bowl with the corn kernels. Sprinkle with the 2 tablespoons flour and 2 tablespoons of the sugar. Stir gently to coat and set aside.

3. Stir together the remaining 1 cup flour, ¾ cup of the sugar, cornmeal, baking powder, baking soda, and salt in a medium bowl. Whisk together the eggs, buttermilk, and olive oil in a small bowl or measuring cup. Stir the egg mixture into the flour mixture just until they are well combined. Gently fold the floured-and-sugared berries and corn into the batter.

4. Pour the batter into the prepared pan and spread evenly. Bake until the top is golden and a toothpick inserted near the center tests clean, 40 to 45 minutes. Let cool in the pan on a wire rack until almost completely cool. Run a thin knife around the inside edge of the pan to loosen the cake sides. Invert a flat plate or baking sheet over the pan and invert the pan and plate together to release the cake. Lift off the pan, then invert the cake again onto a serving plate.

5. A few minutes before serving, toss the reserved berries with the remaining 2 tablespoons sugar. Serve the cake slightly warm or at room temperature. Top each slice with a dollop of whipped cream, if desired, and a scattering of sugared berries.

AVOCADO VELVET

It makes sense that the buttery flesh of the avocado would make the richest, silkiest pudding imaginable. The surprise is that it goes together so easily!

SEASON TO TASTE: You will likely find avocados in farmers' markets in only a handful of states, with California producing the largest U.S. crop. Fortunately, they are easily found in grocery stores. You can vary the topping with local fruits that provide a refreshing balance to this rich dessert, such as strawberries, raspberries, and blackberries; sliced peaches, nectarines, or apricots; or a mix of such tropical fruits as mangoes, kiwifruits, and bananas, cut into bite-size pieces.

1 pound (about 2 large) firm-ripe
    avocados

About 6 tablespoons granulated sugar

2 tablespoons fresh lime juice

⅛ teaspoon kosher salt

1 cup half-and-half, very cold

2 tablespoons water

1 sprig mint, about 3 inches long, plus
    6 mint leaves for garnish

1 pint (about 2 cups) blueberries

Lightly sweetened, softly whipped
    cream, for serving (optional)

1. Cut the avocados in half, discard the pits, and scoop out the flesh, scraping away any brown parts. Measure out 1 cup packed avocado flesh (reserve the rest, if any, for another use) and put into a food processor or blender. Add 3 tablespoons of the sugar, the lime juice, and salt and process until completely smooth. Add the half-and-half and continue processing until the mixture is thick and creamy, like pudding. Taste and add another tablespoon of sugar, if you like. Refrigerate in an airtight container until cold, at least 2 hours or up to 1 day.

2. Stir together the remaining 2 tablespoons sugar and the water in a small saucepan over medium heat until the sugar is completely dissolved. Remove from the heat and stir in the mint sprig. Add ¾ cup of the blueberries and stir gently to coat with the syrup. Set aside at room temperature for up to 1 hour, or refrigerate, covered, for up to 2 days.

3. Gently fold the remaining 1¼ cups blueberries into the cold pudding. Remove the mint sprig from the sugared berries and discard. Stack the mint leaves, roll up tightly lengthwise, and cut crosswise into fine ribbons. Spoon the avocado pudding into four small bowls, and top each serving with a dollop of whipped cream. Using a slotted spoon, spoon the berries over the pudding, then sprinkle with the mint.

∾ FARM JOURNAL ∾

This pudding is best made with the pebbly, dark-skinned Hass variety, which accounts for the lion's share of California's avocado crop and is grown practically year-round. Use avocados that are ripe but not bruised or squishy.

FARMER'S SECRET CHOCOLATE BUNDT CAKE

MAKES

12

SERVINGS

You might be surprised by the number of recipes floating about for chocolate cakes that incorporate vegetables, with raw zucchini and beets the most common additions. But have you seen one with both? Here, the two contribute to a soul-satisfying chocolate cake that stays moist and flavorful for days. Don't be shy to try it. The vegetables "melt" into the cake as it bakes so you never detect them, especially if you peel the zucchini. Even the most ardent beet naysayers love it!

Thanks to passionate Parisian blogger and cookbook author Clotilde Dusoulier for naming her blog Chocolate and Zucchini, which got my mind spinning about combining these two improbable ingredients. Although it wasn't the reason for her blog's name (rather, she was describing two disparate aspects of her cooking style: healthful and natural and chocolate-sweet), Dusoulier later paired the two and was pleased with the result. Many of her readers have written in to say that their grandmothers made such a cake. I guess the idea isn't so crazy new after all.

CAKE

2 cups unbleached all-purpose flour

⅔ cup unsweetened natural cocoa powder (not Dutch processed)

2 teaspoons baking powder

1 teaspoon baking soda

1 teaspoon kosher salt

½ teaspoon ground cinnamon

½ cup (1 stick) unsalted butter, softened

1 cup granulated sugar

½ cup gently packed light brown sugar

3 large eggs, at room temperature

½ cup sour cream or Greek-style plain whole-milk or low-fat yogurt

1 teaspoon pure vanilla extract

1. Preheat the oven to 350°F, with a rack in the lower third. Generously butter a 10-cup Bundt pan. Dust the pan with flour, tapping out the excess. (Alternatively, use a 9-by-2-inch square baking pan.)

2. To make the cake, sift together the flour, cocoa powder, baking powder, baking soda, salt, and cinnamon into a bowl. Set aside.

3. In the bowl of a standing mixer fitted with the paddle attachment (or with a handheld mixer), beat together the butter, granulated sugar, and brown sugar on medium speed until light and creamy, about 5 minutes. Mix in the eggs, one at a time, beating well and stopping and scraping down the bowl after each addition. Mix in the sour cream and vanilla. On low speed, add the flour mixture and beat until nearly combined but still streaky. (The batter will be thick.) Use a wooden spoon or a spatula to stir in the zucchini, beets, and chocolate chips.

4. Transfer the batter to the prepared pan and spread evenly. Bake until a long toothpick or thin wooden skewer inserted midway between the inner and outer edges of the pan tests clean, about 50 minutes. Let cool in the pan on a wire rack for 30 minutes. Using oven mitts if needed, invert a flat serving plate over the pan and invert the pan and plate together to release the cake. Lift off the pan and let cool completely.

1 cup gently packed peeled and grated
   zucchini

1 cup gently packed peeled and finely
   grated red beets

1 cup (6 ounces) semisweet chocolate
   chips

CHOCOLATE GLAZE

⅓ cup heavy cream

3 ounces bittersweet chocolate (60 to
   70 percent cacao), chopped

5. To make the glaze, heat the cream in a small saucepan over medium
    heat until steam begins to rise and bubbles form along the edge of the
    pan. Remove from the heat, add the chocolate, and let stand for 1 min-
    ute, then stir until smooth. Let stand until thick but still pourable,
    10 to 12 minutes. (Rewarm if it gets too thick.)

6. Pour the glaze in a circular motion over the top of the completely
    cooled cake, allowing some to drip down the center and sides. Allow
    the glaze to set for about 1 hour before serving.

7. Store leftover cake, tightly covered, at room temperature for up to
    1 day. Or, refrigerate for up to 5 days, then let stand at room tempera-
    ture for 15 to 30 minutes before serving.

CARROT-ORANGE LAYER CAKE with ORANGE–CRÈME FRAÎCHE FROSTING

MAKES

12

SERVINGS

If you have ever sipped a glowing orange glass of fresh-squeezed carrot-orange juice, you know that these two flavors have a special affinity for each other, each brightening the other. Put the two together and you're well on your way toward five fruits and vegetables for the day.

I developed this cake for a friend's sixtieth birthday, which a group of us celebrated on Cape Cod. What we didn't finish on the day of the party, we consumed for breakfast and snacks over the remaining days of our stay. When we are together back home in California, I'm always asked for a repeat performance.

Use navel oranges, which are seedless, or a variety such as the Hamlin or Valencia that is nearly so. Philadelphia brand cream cheese is your best bet for the frosting, though you can use the same brand's lower-fat Neufchatel, if you prefer. This cake can also be made in a 13-by-9-inch pan.

SEASON TO TASTE: I haven't tried this with zucchini and lemon in place of the carrot and orange, but doesn't that sound good? One lemon might be enough.

CAKE

2 oranges, preferably organic

3 cups gently packed peeled and grated carrots

1½ cups unbleached all-purpose flour

½ cup whole-wheat pastry flour or white whole-wheat flour

2 teaspoons baking powder

1½ teaspoons baking soda

1 teaspoon kosher salt

½ teaspoon ground cinnamon

4 large eggs

1 cup granulated sugar

½ cup gently packed light brown sugar

CONTINUED >

1. Preheat the oven to 350°F, with one rack in the upper third and one rack in the lower third. Coat two 8-by-2-inch round cake pans with oil. Dust the pans with flour, tapping out the excess.

2. To make the cake, finely grate 1 tablespoon plus 1 teaspoon zest from the oranges. Peel the oranges, discarding the skin and trimming away any visible white pith. Cut the oranges in half and, if they are not navels, poke out any seeds. Put the oranges in a food processor or blender and pulse until they are in small chunks. Transfer to a bowl and stir in 1 tablespoon of the orange zest and all of the carrots. (Set aside the remaining 1 teaspoon zest for the frosting.)

3. Stir together the all-purpose flour, whole-wheat flour, baking powder, baking soda, salt, and cinnamon in a small bowl. Whisk together the eggs, granulated sugar, brown sugar, sour cream, oil, and vanilla in a large bowl until well combined. Stir the flour mixture into the egg mixture just until blended. Using a spatula or large spoon, stir in the carrot-orange mixture (including any juice in the bowl) and the pecans.

CONTINUED >

½ cup sour cream

½ cup canola or grapeseed oil

½ teaspoon pure vanilla extract

1 cup pecans, toasted and coarsely
chopped

FROSTING

12 ounces cream cheese, softened

½ cup (1 stick) unsalted butter,
softened

2 cups confectioners' sugar

¾ cup crème fraîche or sour cream,
cold

½ teaspoon pure vanilla extract

Pinch of kosher salt

1 teaspoon orange zest (reserved from
cake preparation)

Finely chopped, toasted pecans, for
decorating (optional)

4. Divide the batter evenly between the prepared pans. Bake until a toothpick inserted near the center of a cake layer tests clean, about 40 minutes, switching the pans between the racks and rotating them front to back about halfway through baking. Let cool completely in the pans on wire racks.

5. While the cake layers bake, make the frosting, which will need time to chill. Beat together the cream cheese and butter with a handheld electric mixer on medium speed until smooth. On low speed, gradually add the confectioners' sugar and beat until combined, stopping to scrape down the bowl as needed. Add the crème fraîche, vanilla, salt, and the reserved 1 teaspoon orange zest and beat just until smooth. Increase the speed to medium and beat until thick and creamy, about 15 seconds. Do not overmix. Cover and refrigerate until firm enough to spread, 30 to 60 minutes.

6. Run a thin knife around the inside edge of each pan to loosen the cake sides. Invert a flat serving plate over one pan and invert the pan and plate together to release the cake. Lift off the pan. Spread about one-third of the frosting evenly over the top. (An offset spatula is the best tool for this task.) Invert the second layer onto a plate in the same fashion, then place, top-side up, over the frosted layer. Spread the remaining frosting over the top and sides of the cake, swirling it decoratively if you like. Press the chopped pecans onto the sides of the cake, or in a ring around the top perimeter of the cake, if desired.

7. Refrigerate for at least 30 minutes to set the frosting, or up to 3 days, covering the cake after the frosting has set. It is equally good served directly from the refrigerator or at room temperature.

MOJITO MELON BALLS

These refreshing mouthfuls of melon bathed in mint, lime, and rum are the perfect way to cool down on a hot summer day. I like to double the mint syrup and refrigerate half of it in a sealed jar to perk up iced tea or other fruits. This dessert is best served the day it is made.

SEASON TO TASTE: Substitute locally available melons and experiment with herbs from your market or your own garden. For a refreshing red, white, and blue finish to a Fourth of July barbecue, use watermelon and a white-fleshed melon and add blueberries.

½ cup granulated sugar

½ cup water

⅓ cup firmly packed fresh spearmint leaves or mixed mint and lemon verbena leaves, coarsely chopped, plus 8 mint leaves for garnish

2 tablespoons light rum (optional)

1 personal-size seedless watermelon, or ¼ large seedless watermelon

1 small to medium Crenshaw, Sharlyn, honeydew, Charantais, cantaloupe, or other melon

Finely grated zest and juice of 1 lime, plus 1 lime for garnish

1. Bring the sugar and water to a boil in a small saucepan over medium heat, swirling the pan to dissolve the sugar. Boil for about 1 minute until the sugar is completely dissolved, then remove from the heat and stir in the ⅓ cup mint leaves and rum (if using). Let cool to room temperature, about 20 minutes.

2. While the syrup cools, cut the melons in half. Using a melon baller, scoop out 8 cups of melon balls, placing them in a large bowl. (Alternatively, cut the melon into about ½-inch cubes.)

3. Pour the cooled syrup through a fine-mesh strainer held over the melon balls, pressing on the leaves to extract as much flavor as possible. Add the lime zest and juice and toss to coat. Cover tightly and refrigerate until very cold.

4. Toss the melon balls again to coat. Scoop the balls into dessert glasses along with a spoonful or two of the juices. Stack the mint leaves for garnish, roll up tightly lengthwise, and cut crosswise into fine ribbons. Thinly slice the lime crosswise into rings. Just before serving, scatter the mint over the melon and decorate with the lime slices.

RHUBARB, BLUEBERRY & CREAM PARFAIT

MAKES

SERVINGS

This is the perfect red, white, and blueberry dessert to celebrate the Fourth of July, or the entire blueberry-rhubarb season, which runs from about May to July. Depending on your location, Independence Day should hit close to the end of the blueberry season, just in time for a final celebration of that bright berry's bursting fireworks of flavor.

The crunchy topping is a great complement to the smooth cream and rhubarb. It is also a delicious topping for ice cream and fresh fruit. Alternatively, you can use granola or crumble your favorite gingersnaps over the parfaits. The crunch topping and rhubarb can be prepared in advance for a quick-fix dessert.

SEASON TO TASTE: Substitute strawberries or raspberries for the rhubarb, reducing the sugar to ¼ cup. Or, substitute blackberries or olallieberries for the blueberries.

RHUBARB SAUCE

½ cup granulated sugar

2 tablespoons water

1 pound rhubarb (about 4 medium to large stalks), leaves discarded and stalks cut into ½-inch pieces

Small pinch of kosher salt

1 teaspoon fresh lime juice

CRUNCH TOPPING

½ cup unbleached all-purpose flour

¼ cup old-fashioned rolled oats

⅓ cup gently packed light brown sugar

1½ teaspoons ground ginger

¼ teaspoon kosher salt

½ teaspoon pure vanilla extract

4 tablespoons (½ stick) unsalted butter, cold, cut into 8 pieces

CONTINUED >

1. To make the sauce, stir together the sugar and water in a large non-reactive saucepan over medium heat until the sugar is completely dissolved. Add the rhubarb and stir to coat with the sugar syrup. Reduce the heat to a slow simmer, cover, and cook until the fruit is quite soft, about 10 minutes. Remove from the heat. Process until smooth using an immersion blender or standard blender, or mash and stir with a fork. Stir in the salt and lime juice, then taste and adjust with sugar or lime, if needed. (It will taste sweeter chilled than hot.) Let cool to room temperature, then refrigerate in a covered container until cold, at least 2 hours or up to 2 days.

2. To make the topping, stir together the flour, oats, brown sugar, ginger, and salt in a bowl. Sprinkle the vanilla evenly over the mixture, then scatter the butter over the mixture. Using your fingertips, rub in the butter until the mixture looks like wet, clumpy sand. Scatter the almonds over the top and mix them in with your fingers. Cover and refrigerate the topping for 30 minutes.

3. While the topping chills, preheat the oven to 375°F, with a rack near the center. Line a rimmed baking sheet with a silicone baking mat or parchment paper.

CONTINUED >

½ cup sliced almonds

½ cup heavy cream

½ cup crème fraîche or sour cream

2 teaspoons granulated sugar

1 pint (2 cups) blueberries

4. Use your fingers to crumble the topping mixture onto the baking sheet. It should look like granola, with a few larger clumps. Bake until golden brown, 15 to 20 minutes, stirring and turning with a spatula once or twice during baking. Let cool completely before using. (It will keep in an airtight container at room temperature for up to 1 week.)

5. Using a chilled bowl and beaters, whip together the cream, crème fraîche, and sugar until the mixture holds medium-firm peaks.

6. Layer the cream, rhubarb, crunch topping, and berries in four parfait glasses. As a guide—without worrying about using exact quantities—divide one-third of the cream among the four glasses. Layer half of the rhubarb sauce over the cream. Sprinkle about 1 tablespoon of the topping into each glass. Then, sprinkle one-third of the berries over the topping in the four glasses. Repeat the layers, using half of the remaining cream, all of the remaining rhubarb, about 1 tablespoon of crunch topping for each glass, and half of the remaining berries. Top the parfaits evenly with the remaining cream, and then sprinkle evenly with the remaining berries. Finally, sprinkle lightly with some crunch topping. (You will have some crunch topping remaining.)

7. Serve immediately, or cover tightly and refrigerate for up to 24 hours. The crunch will soften but will still add great flavor and texture.

MAUI PINEAPPLE-MACADAMIA UPSIDE-DOWN CAKE

MAKES

8-10

SERVINGS

Ah, Maui, where macadamia nuts can be found alongside pineapples and coconuts at many farmers' markets. Fortunately for mainlanders, the ingredients are readily available, although not at the local farmers' market. You can get away with using packaged coconut and macadamia nuts (preferably from Maui), but don't compromise on the pineapple. You will need a cast-iron skillet or other heavy pan made for both the stove top and the oven.

SEASON TO TASTE: Substitute pitted apricot halves for the pineapple and toasted slivered blanched almonds for the macadamia nuts, or try sliced pears and chopped toasted pecans. Substitute apricot or pear brandy for the rum and eliminate the coconut.

TOPPING

4 tablespoons (½ stick) unsalted butter

½ cup firmly packed light brown sugar

2 tablespoons dark rum (optional)

1 small pineapple, peeled, cored, and cut into ½-inch-thick rounds or half rounds

CAKE

1½ cups unbleached all-purpose flour

2 teaspoons baking powder

½ teaspoon kosher salt

½ cup (1 stick) unsalted butter, softened

¾ cup granulated sugar

2 large eggs, at room temperature

½ teaspoon pure vanilla extract

1 cup whole milk

1. Preheat the oven to 350°F, with a rack in the center. Place a sheet of aluminum foil on the rack beneath to catch any dripping caramel.

2. To make the topping, put the butter, brown sugar, and rum (if using) in a 10-inch round cast-iron skillet over medium heat and whisk to melt the sugar and make a smooth sauce. Remove from the heat and arrange the pineapple in the skillet in whatever artistic pattern you like. (It will be the top when you unmold the cake.) Return the pan to medium heat and cook until the caramel bubbles up around the pineapple, about 5 minutes. Remove from the heat and set aside.

3. To make the cake, whisk together the flour, baking powder, and salt in a bowl. Set aside.

4. In the bowl of a standing mixer fitted with the paddle attachment (or with a handheld mixer), beat together the butter and granulated sugar on medium speed until light and creamy, about 5 minutes. Mix in the eggs, one at a time, and then the vanilla, beating well and stopping and scraping down the bowl after each addition. On low speed, add half of the flour mixture, then all of the milk, and then the remaining flour mixture, beating just until combined after each addition. Stop to scrape down the bowl as needed. Set aside 2 tablespoons of the coconut for garnish, then, using a large spatula, fold the remaining coconut and the macadamia nuts into the batter.

¾ cup unsweetened shredded dried coconut or freshly grated coconut, toasted

¾ cup macadamia nuts, toasted and coarsely chopped

Ice cream or lightly sweetened, softly whipped cream, for serving (optional)

5. Pour the batter evenly over the pineapple in the skillet in a spiral, moving from the outside to the middle, to prevent the batter from pushing the caramel to the edges. Smooth the top with the spatula. Bake until a toothpick inserted near the center tests clean, about 40 minutes. Transfer to the stove top to cool for 15 minutes before unmolding.

6. Run a thin knife around the inside edge of the pan to loosen the cake sides. Invert a flat serving plate over the skillet. Using oven mitts, grasp the plate and skillet tightly together on both sides and quickly invert the plate and skillet to release the cake onto the plate. It should fall out easily. If it does not, tap the bottom of the skillet to release the cake, then lift off the skillet. Scrape any remaining caramelized juices from the pan over the cake, and adjust any pineapple slices that may have slipped out of position.

7. Sprinkle the top with the reserved coconut and serve warm or at room temperature, cut into wedges and topped with ice cream, if desired.

8. Refrigerate leftover cake, tightly wrapped, for up to 2 days. Bring to room temperature to serve.

Sweetening the Pot:
HONEY,
Maple Syrup
&
Market Jam

Sweet is what dessert is all about, but there are a number of ways to sweeten a dessert. Honey is available at many farmers' markets, and though it may be produced seasonally, you are likely to find it year-round, at least as long as supplies last. Maple syrup is also produced seasonally and may be available for only a few months after production.

The flavor of honey varies widely, from mild and sweet to robust and bittersweet, and the color from nearly clear to amber to deep brown. The flavor is largely dependent on the plants the bees fed on while gathering their pollen, with some honey tasting uncannily like its pollen source. Honey may be made from a single source, such as acacia, buckwheat, or blackberry blossoms, or a combination of several sources, such as a wildflower mix. According to the United States National Honey Board, more than three hundred unique types of honey are available around the country, each originating from a different floral source. The board's Honey Locator can help you find honey in forty-seven U.S. states and twenty-eight other countries.

Pairing honey with other flavors is a little like matching food with wine. The most reliable way to get it right is by tasting the honey with the major flavor elements in the recipe, such as fruits, nuts, or cheese, to see whether you like them together. Like other pairings, there is no correct answer. It's all about personal preference.

In addition to liquid honey in the jar or honey bear, the most common form, you will find the honeybees' edible wax comb at many markets. Some producers drop chunks of honeycomb into jars of liquid honey to make cut comb honey. Whipped honey is made smooth and spreadable by a controlled process that creates even, fine crystals. Despite sometimes being labeled "creamed" honey, it has no added dairy.

Spencer and Helene Marshall of Marshall's Farm Natural Honey place hives in seventy locations throughout the greater Bay Area to collect their wide variety of honeys. They bottle their raw, unfiltered honey at Marshall's Honey House in American Canyon, at the southern end of California's Napa Valley. More than sixty varieties are listed on their Web site, and all vary widely in taste.

Like honey, maple syrup, which is made from the concentrated sap of maple trees, adds both sweetness and flavor to recipes. Canada is a primary producer, and Vermont, New York, Wisconsin, Ohio, Michigan, Pennsylvania, Maine, and New Hampshire are the largest maple syrup–producing states on this side of the border. Making the syrup is a labor-intensive process, with about forty gallons of sap required for each gallon of syrup. Depending on the location, the season may run from late February through April, with the sap running for only about a month when the temperature conditions are just right.

Claude Richmond of Two Rivers, Wisconsin, started making maple syrup in 1987, after retiring as a firefighter. For Richmond, the work begins in mid-March, when he drills small holes into each maple tree and plugs in metal spigots. He hangs a ten-quart bucket onto each spigot and lets the sap drip in. It takes a freezing night followed by a daytime temperature of 40° to 45°F for the sap to run well, and a few days to fill a bucket. He gets about five "runs" over the course of a season.

The sap is almost clear, like water. After the leaves bud, the sap will turn cloudy, compromising the flavor. Richmond boils the syrup to 219°F on his wood stove, using electric sensors to monitor the temperature. To finish the syrup, he transfers it to a gas stove for more control, then pumps the syrup into a tank, through a pressure filter, and into a bottler. The syrup averages 2.4 percent sugar on a hydrometer, but Richmond says it is best at 3 percent.

Richmond thinks his hardwood trees produce better syrup than the softwood ones, but there's no easy way to tell one type from the other on his twenty-six-acre stand of sugar maples. Hard or soft, the trees provide gorgeous autumn color as the leaves turn brilliant shades of yellow, orange, and red. Their syrup is equally outstanding.

Another way to add flavor and sweetness in tandem to recipes is by incorporating jams, jellies, and preserves. Many farmers produce them using fruit that has become too ripe to sell or with blemishes that don't affect flavor. While these fruit preserves are perfect on a piece of morning toast, they also present opportunities for desserts, baked into buttery thumbprint cookies or served as a topping for soft, fresh cheese, for example.

Selecting and Storing Honey, Maple Syrup, and Jam

The best way to select honey is by tasting it. When that isn't possible, look to its color as a clue to its assertiveness, with the lightest generally being mild and the darkest the most robust. Choose a mild-flavored honey when you want to add sweetness but not significantly alter the flavor of a dessert. Examples include alfalfa and clover and, in the southeastern United States, tupelo. Moderately assertive honeys like wildflower and blackberry are best for contributing flavor without overpowering the dessert. Use a robust honey such as buckwheat or the slightly bitter almond blossom when you want its flavor to stand out in a recipe. Avocado honey is the choice for adding rich, buttery notes.

Potent honeys like chestnut will overtake almost any flavor, making them the perfect choice when you want their flavor to shine strongly through. One caution: do not feed honey to children under one year of age, including baked goods that contain honey, because of the presence of bacterial spores that can cause infant botulism.

Store honey at room temperature in a dark cabinet for up to 2 years. There is no harm in using honey that has crystallized. If you prefer, you can dissolve the crystals by immersing the closed honey jar in hot water up to its fill line, or by heating it in a microwave oven just until the crystals melt.

The United States Department of Agriculture requires that maple syrup be graded A and qualified Light, Medium, or Dark Amber, or B, which is sometimes labeled cooking syrup. (Vermont uses a slightly different system.) Produced from the season's first sap, Grade A Light Amber (called Vermont Fancy in Vermont) has the lightest color and most delicate flavor. It is also the priciest. I prefer the more deeply flavored Grade B or Grade A Dark Amber syrup for baking, although any of them will work well in these recipes. Always opt for pure maple syrup over imitation maple syrup or pancake syrup, which bear little resemblance to the real thing.

Store unopened containers of maple syrup in a cool, dark pantry for up to 1 year and refrigerate after opening. I found no guidelines for how long the syrup can be refrigerated safely, but many producers recommend freezing it for long-term storage. It will become more viscous but should remain pourable.

For use in desserts, select jams, jellies, and preserves by taste, complementing or contrasting them with other flavors in the dessert. Although shelf life varies widely, a good guideline is to store unopened jars in a cool, dark pantry for up to 1 year, and refrigerate after opening for use within 1 month.

HONEYCOMB CHEESE PLATE WITH ROSEMARY CORNMEAL CRISPS

MAKES

6

SERVINGS

Honeycomb is the centerpiece of this dramatic cheese plate, which offers all the best characteristics of a good dessert: rich, sweet, a little salty, and full of enticing textures and flavors. Invite guests to cut a piece of honeycomb (it is entirely edible) and place it atop a crisp wafer along with the cheese. If you can't find honeycomb, pour a flavorful, local honey into a shallow dish and set a honey dipper or small spoon in it.

Consider including one goat's milk cheese, such as a crottin or fresh chèvre; a firm or semi-firm sheep's milk cheese, such as Manchego or Ossau-Iraty; and a blue-veined cheese, such as Valdéon, Cabrales, or Point Reyes Farmstead Cheese Company's Original Blue.

Crunchy and aromatic, with hints of rosemary and black pepper and a touch of sweetness, the addictive crisps sew together the earthy, salty, sweet, and nutty elements on the plate. They come together quickly, and are infinitely more enjoyable than store-bought crackers. If you prefer, substitute whole-grain crackers, thin spice cookies, or thin slices of nut bread. Dates & Figs with Fromage Blanc & Toasted Nuts (page 98) are a wonderful addition to the fruits on the platter.

CORNMEAL CRISPS

½ cup fine or medium stone-ground yellow cornmeal

¼ cup whole-wheat flour

1 tablespoon granulated sugar

Heaping ½ teaspoon finely chopped fresh rosemary needles

¼ teaspoon kosher salt

¼ teaspoon baking soda

⅛ teaspoon freshly ground black pepper

¼ cup buttermilk or plain low-fat yogurt

4 teaspoons extra virgin olive oil

CONTINUED >

1. Preheat the oven to 350°F, with a rack in the lower third. Turn a 17-by-12-inch rimmed baking sheet upside down and cover the bottom with a silicone baking mat or a sheet of parchment paper.

2. To make the crisps, stir together the cornmeal, flour, sugar, a generous ¼ teaspoon of the rosemary, kosher salt, baking soda, and pepper in a bowl. Mix in the buttermilk and oil with a wooden spoon, then gather the dough with your hands and knead it in the bowl just a turn or two to bring it together into a ball.

3. Center the dough on the prepared baking sheet and press it into as large a rectangle as you can easily form using your hands. Cover with a piece of plastic film the size of the baking sheet. Roll lengthwise from the center to the edges of the dough, alternating one direction and then the other and avoiding rolling over the ends, until the dough evenly covers the entire baking sheet. (With some patience it will reach the right size.)

CONTINUED >

⅛ teaspoon Maldon sea salt or kosher salt, for finishing

Piece of honeycomb, about 6 ounces

Selection of 2 or 3 cheeses, about 1 pound total

Marcona or regular almonds or other nuts, toasted and lightly salted

Fresh and dried figs, dates, apricots, cherries, and/or golden raisins

4. Carefully peel off the top sheet of film, and press the dough with your fingertips to patch any holes. Using a pizza wheel or a sharp knife, score (no need to cut clear through) the dough lengthwise into six equal strips. Then score crosswise into ten equal strips.

5. Mix together the remaining ¼ teaspoon rosemary and the sea salt in a small dish. Mist the dough very lightly with water, using a spray bottle or spritzing with wet fingers. Scatter the rosemary and salt mixture evenly over the top.

6. Bake until the sheet of crisps is toasty golden brown all over (the edges will be slightly darker), 10 to 12 minutes, keeping a watchful eye toward the end to prevent burning and rotating the pan front to back a little past halfway through baking. Remove from the oven and immediately flip the pan onto a flat, dry surface. Wait for 30 seconds, then lift off the pan and peel off the mat or paper. Let the sheet of crisps stand until cool, just a few minutes. Break the crisps apart at the score marks. Store the completely cooled crisps in an airtight container at room temperature for up to 4 days.

7. Place the honeycomb in the center of a large serving platter, and arrange the cheeses around it. Scatter the nuts and fruit around the platter to make an attractive presentation. Include the crisps on the platter, or serve in a basket or bowl on the side.

∾ FARM JOURNAL ∾

At Tairwá-Knoll Farms in Brentwood, California, Rick and Kristie Knoll make good use of the space between rows of fig and apricot trees by growing wide swaths of rosemary. Most of the herb goes to bakeries and restaurants for breads, including the wonderful herb slab made by Acme Bread Company in Berkeley, California.

OVEN-STEAMED PERSIMMON PUDDING WITH HONEY-LEMON HARD SAUCE

MAKES

10–12

SERVINGS

I have been making this recipe, an adaptation of a favorite from Marion Cunningham, for the holidays since I discovered it in 1982. Hers is steamed in a coffee can or pudding mold set on a rack in a pot of simmering water. But then, when was the last time you saw coffee in a can? A few ingredient changes later, this version is baked in a covered casserole, allowing steam to build up inside so the pudding emerges equally moist and delectable.

There's nothing difficult or rigid about the sauce: "hard" refers to the addition of rum, which provides a boost of flavor in both the pudding and sauce.

PUDDING

3 to 4 very ripe Hachiya persimmons

1 teaspoon baking soda

½ cup unbleached all-purpose flour

½ cup white whole-wheat flour, whole-wheat pastry flour, or additional unbleached all-purpose flour

1 teaspoon baking powder

1 teaspoon ground cinnamon

½ teaspoon kosher salt

¼ teaspoon freshly grated mace or nutmeg

⅓ cup dried currants or golden raisins

⅓ cup pecans or walnuts, toasted and coarsely chopped

2 tablespoons finely chopped crystallized ginger

2 large eggs

⅔ cup firmly packed light brown sugar

½ cup buttermilk

¼ cup canola or other neutral vegetable oil

1. Preheat the oven to 350°F, with a rack in the lower third. Oil a 2-quart covered casserole.

2. To make the pudding, use a paring knife to carve out the calyx (hard top) from each persimmon (as you would core a tomato). Use a spoon to scrape the pulp into a blender or food processor, discarding the thin skin and seed, if there is one. Process to break up the pulps until smooth. Measure 1 cup puree into a bowl. (Save any remaining puree for another use.) Stir in the baking soda. Set aside.

3. Whisk together the all-purpose flour, whole-wheat flour, baking powder, cinnamon, salt, and mace in a small bowl. Stir in the currants, nuts, and ginger.

4. Whisk the persimmon mixture, which will have become very stiff, to break it up. Whisk in the eggs, brown sugar, buttermilk, oil, rum, and lemon juice until well combined. Stir in the flour mixture just until it is incorporated.

5. Pour the batter into the prepared casserole. Cover and bake until a toothpick inserted into the center tests clean, about 55 minutes. Set aside, still covered, to cool slightly, at least 20 minutes.

6. To make the hard sauce, stir together the confectioners' sugar, honey, and butter in a bowl until well blended. Stir in the lemon zest and juice, rum, and salt to make a creamy sauce.

2 tablespoons dark rum

1 tablespoon fresh lemon juice

HARD SAUCE

½ cup confectioners' sugar

¼ cup mild-flavored honey, such as acacia, alfalfa, or clover

4 tablespoons (½ stick) unsalted butter, softened

Finely grated zest of 1 lemon

2 tablespoons fresh lemon juice

1 tablespoon dark rum

¼ teaspoon kosher salt

7. Scoop the warm pudding into bowls and top with the hard sauce.

8. Refrigerate leftover pudding in the covered casserole for up to 4 days. Heat in a conventional or microwave oven until just warm before serving. Refrigerate leftover hard sauce, tightly covered, for up to 3 days and bring to room temperature to serve.

∾ FARM JOURNAL ∾

I get my Hachiya persimmons from my English neighbor's tree. She insists they have nothing of the kind in England and has no idea what to do with them. It doesn't get much more local than that!

ROASTED PUMPKIN PIE IN A MAPLE-PECAN CRUST

MAKES

SERVINGS

Jack-o'-lanterns are great for carving, but for pie, you want a firm-fleshed, sweet pumpkin without a lot of tough fibers. Pie pumpkins are typically labeled Sugar Pie, New England Sugar, or simply sugar or pie pumpkins. Making a pie with a fresh pumpkin may seem like a lot of extra steps, but your efforts will be well rewarded. To save a step, purchase a store-bought crust, but in the spirit of the market, try making your own pumpkin puree.

The crust and the roasted pumpkin can both be made up to a day in advance. The dough needs time to chill twice: once before rolling and once after.

SEASON TO TASTE: Substitute butternut or kabocha squash (also known as Japanese pumpkin) for the pumpkin. The pie made from the kabocha will be lighter in color and have an alluring sweet flavor reminiscent of chestnuts. Or, follow the lead of recipe tester Sara Goepfrich, who couldn't find pumpkin or squash in the depths of a Mishawaka, Indiana winter. Sara used Garnet yams (actually a type of sweet potato), straining the filling before pouring it into the pie shell, and raved about the result. You will need only 2 pounds.

CRUST

¼ cup pecans, toasted

1¼ cups unbleached all-purpose flour

½ teaspoon kosher salt

1 tablespoon maple syrup, cold

½ cup (1 stick) unsalted butter, cold, cut into 8 pieces

About 1 tablespoon ice water

FILLING

One 3- to 4-pound pie pumpkin

1½ cups half-and-half

½ cup gently packed light brown sugar

CONTINUED >

1. To make the crust, put the pecans and ¼ cup of the flour in a food processor and pulse until the pecans are finely chopped. Add the remaining 1 cup flour, salt, and maple syrup and pulse a few times to combine. Scatter the butter over the top and pulse until the butter is in pieces that vary in size from oat flakes to small peas. Drizzle in about 1½ teaspoons ice water and pulse to combine until a lump of dough pinched between your fingers holds together. If not, add a little more ice water and try again.

2. When the dough is ready, turn it out onto a sheet of plastic film. Gather it into a ball, flatten the ball into a disk, wrap, and refrigerate for at least 30 minutes or up to 1 day.

3. Place the dough disk between two sheets of lightly floured plastic film and roll out into a 13-inch circle. Peel off the top sheet. Then, using the bottom sheet, flip the dough circle over a 10-inch pie pan. Carefully peel off the second sheet of film. (If it is difficult to peel, refrigerate for 15 minutes and try again.) Lift and fit the dough snugly onto the sides and bottom of the pan. Tuck the overhanging

CONTINUED >

¼ cup pure maple syrup

3 large eggs

1 large egg yolk

1 teaspoon finely grated fresh ginger

1 teaspoon ground cinnamon

½ teaspoon kosher salt

¼ teaspoon ground cardamom

⅛ teaspoon finely ground white pepper

1 egg white, lightly beaten with
    2 teaspoons water, for brushing
    crust

Lightly sweetened, softly whipped
    cream, for serving

DRESSING UP YOUR PIE

To decorate the pie, pinch off a small piece of dough before rolling the crust. Roll out on a floured surface, and use a maple leaf or pumpkin cookie cutter to cut one large or two or three smaller shapes. Brush with the egg white wash when you brush the crust, sprinkle with coarse sugar, and bake on a lightly oiled baking sheet beside the pie until golden, about 20 minutes. Place on top of the cooled pie before serving.

dough under to form a double-thick rim, then pinch the dough rim between your thumb and index finger to form a fluted edge. Cover loosely with plastic film and refrigerate for at least 1 hour or up to 1 day.

4. Preheat the oven to 375°F, with a rack in the lower third. Oil a rimmed baking sheet.

5. To make the filling, cut the pumpkin in half around the equator. Scrape out the seeds and strings from the inside. Lay the pumpkin, cut-side down, on the prepared baking sheet. Bake until very soft, 1 to 1½ hours, depending on the size. Set aside until cool enough to handle.

6. Scoop the pumpkin flesh into a food processor and process until completely smooth. Measure out 2 cups of the puree and return to the food processor. (Any remaining puree makes a nice side dish with the addition of a little butter, salt, and a drizzle of maple syrup.) Add the half-and-half, brown sugar, maple syrup, eggs, egg yolk, ginger, cinnamon, salt, cardamom, and pepper. Process until smooth and well combined.

7. Preheat the oven to 400°F, with a rack near the center and a rimless baking sheet centered on the rack.

8. Prick the bottom and sides of the chilled crust all over with a fork. Brush the bottom and sides with the egg white wash and then dab a little of the wash along the fluted edge. Pour the filling into the crust.

9. Bake on the preheated baking sheet until the filling is puffed and jiggles just slightly in the center when you gently shake the pan, about 1 hour. (Protect the crust with aluminum foil if it browns too quickly before the filling is done.) Let cool completely on a wire rack, at least 1 hour. Refrigerate until cold, at least several hours or up to 3 days. To avoid condensation, cover tightly with plastic film only after completely cold.

10. Cut into wedges and top each slice with a dollop of whipped cream.

APPLES & HONEY BUNDT CAKE

MAKES

12

SERVINGS

This cake is perfect for Rosh Hashanah, the Jewish New Year, when apples are traditionally dipped into a bowl of honey to augur a sweet year. The moist, nut-studded cake soaked in honey and cider syrup keeps extraordinarily well—in fact, it gets even better with time. Wrapped tightly, it can be refrigerated for up to a week or frozen for up to a month. Be sure to bring it to room temperature before serving.

Use tart, flavorful apples such as Granny Smith, pippin, or Gravenstein, or better yet, ask your market vendor what's best. Choose a flavorful honey, too—and dip a slice of apple into it to be sure you like their flavors together. Whole-milk or low-fat yogurt or sour cream can be substituted for the buttermilk.

SEASON TO TASTE: Try pears and pecans in place of the apples and walnuts.

CAKE

2½ cups unbleached all-purpose flour

½ cup whole-wheat flour

1½ teaspoons baking soda

1 teaspoon ground cinnamon

½ teaspoon ground cardamom

1 teaspoon kosher salt

1 cup canola, grapeseed, or other
neutral vegetable oil

1 cup gently packed light brown sugar

¼ cup buttermilk

¼ cup moderately assertive to robust
honey, such as almond blossom,
orange blossom, or buckwheat

3 large eggs

1 teaspoon pure vanilla extract

3 cups peeled, cored, and cubed apples
(½-inch cubes; about 3 apples)

1. Preheat the oven to 350°F, with a rack near the center. Butter a 10- to 12-cup Bundt pan. Dust with flour, tapping out the excess.

2. To make the cake, whisk together the all-purpose flour, whole-wheat flour, baking soda, cinnamon, cardamom, and salt in a bowl. Set aside.

3. Whisk together the oil, brown sugar, buttermilk, honey, eggs, and vanilla in a large bowl until well blended. Stir in the flour mixture, mixing just until streaky. Fold in the apples and nuts until everything is evenly combined. The batter will be thick.

4. Spread the batter evenly in the prepared pan. Bake until a long toothpick or thin wooden skewer inserted midway between the inner and outer edges of the pan tests clean, about 45 minutes. Let cool on a wire rack for 25 minutes. Using oven mitts if the pan is still hot to the touch, invert the warm cake onto a serving plate.

5. While the cake cools, make the syrup. Combine the cider, honey, and butter in a small saucepan over medium heat and boil until reduced to about ⅓ cup, about 15 minutes.

6. Prick the warm cake all over with a thin wooden skewer or toothpick, then brush the cake with the syrup until it absorbs all of it.

7. Serve slightly warm or at room temperature.

1 cup chopped toasted walnuts

SYRUP

¼ cup apple cider (unfiltered apple juice)

¼ cup honey (same type as for cake or one with a complementary flavor)

2 tablespoons unsalted butter

∾ FARM JOURNAL ∽

Marshall's Farm Natural Honey in American Canyon, California, sells an almond blossom honey that is out of this world in this cake. It lends a subtle bittersweet note that somehow fits perfectly with the solemn-sweet spirit of the holiday. Helene Marshall packages several products specially for Jewish holidays, including the charmingly labeled "Rosh Hashanah in a Jar," a mix of dried apples and raw, unfiltered honey.

MAPLE SYRUP COFFEE POTS DE CRÈME

MAKES

6

SERVINGS

Unless you live in Hawaii or another coffee-growing region, you won't find locally grown coffee at your farmers' market. But more and more, you will find a coffee vendor, sometimes with locally roasted coffee beans purchased from a fair trade supplier. Look for a medium roast, either regular or decaffeinated. For the best flavor and texture, use cream free of emulsifiers and additives and not ultrapasteurized.

A *pot de crème* is a little covered porcelain pot traditionally used to serve a rich custard of the same name. These custards are nice served with a crisp cookie, such as Hazelnut-Almond Biscotti (page 191) or Lavender Walnut Sandies (page 194). Think of the pot de crème as a good, strong, sweet cup of coffee to accompany the cookies!

2 cups heavy cream

½ cup whole milk

½ cup plus 2 teaspoons pure maple syrup

¼ cup medium-roast coffee beans, cracked with a knife or pulsed briefly in a coffee grinder

½ vanilla bean, split lengthwise

1 large egg

4 large egg yolks

¼ teaspoon kosher salt

¼ teaspoon medium-roast coffee ground for an espresso machine (very fine), plus more for garnish

1. Refrigerate ½ cup of the cream for the topping. Warm the remaining 1½ cups cream, the milk, ½ cup maple syrup, cracked coffee beans, and the vanilla bean in a small nonreactive saucepan over medium heat until steam rises from the surface and bubbles begin to form along the edge of the pan. Remove from the heat and set aside to steep for 30 minutes.

2. Preheat the oven to 300°F, with a rack in the lower third. Use a baking pan at least 2 inches deep and large enough to hold six 4-ounce pot de crème pots, ovenproof cappuccino cups, or ramekins without crowding. Line the pan with a folded kitchen towel to prevent the molds from sliding, and place the molds in the pan, spacing them evenly. Bring a kettle of water to a boil and remove from the heat.

3. Whisk together the egg, egg yolks, salt, and the ¼ teaspoon ground coffee in a bowl, preferably one with a spout, until well combined. Whisking continuously, gradually pour the steeped cream mixture through a fine-mesh strainer into the egg mixture until well combined. Retrieve the vanilla bean from the strainer and, using a paring knife, scrape the seeds from the bean into the custard mixture, then stir to disperse them. Discard the bean.

4. Ladle or pour the custard into the molds, dividing it evenly. Put the pan on the oven rack, and pour the hot water from the kettle into the pan until it reaches one-third of the way to halfway up the sides

CONTINUED >

of the molds, taking care not to splash water into the custards. Cover the *pot de crème* pots with their lids, or drape a single piece of aluminum foil over all of the molds.

5. Bake until the custards are set around the edges but jiggle slightly in the middle when you gently shake a mold, about 35 minutes for small molds and as long as 1 hour for deep ramekins. As the custards set, use oven mitts and a flexible metal spatula to transfer the molds to a wire rack. Let cool for 30 minutes.

6. Refrigerate the custards until thoroughly chilled, at least 2 hours or up to 4 days. To avoid condensation, cover tightly with plastic film only after completely cold.

7. Using a chilled bowl and a chilled whisk or beaters, whip the remaining ½ cup cream with the remaining 2 teaspoons maple syrup until the cream holds medium-firm peaks. Pile the cream on top of the custards and sprinkle a pinch of ground coffee over each serving.

MARKET JAM GEMS

MAKES ABOUT

5

DOZEN COOKIES

Whether you purchase jams and jellies from a purveyor at the market or make your own from market fruit, these diminutive, buttery, jam-filled cookies are just the thing for showcasing your favorite preserves. It is worth using the best-quality butter, as well.

For rustic cookies, leave any small pieces of fruit from the preserves in the filling. For the most refined cookies, heat jam or preserves in a small saucepan over low heat just until melted, then pass through a fine-mesh strainer into a small bowl, pressing on the solids to extract as much of the fruit essence as possible. Let cool before filling the cookies.

SEASON TO TASTE: Make a batch with a variety of fillings. Or, roll the balls in lightly beaten egg white and then in finely ground almonds or walnuts before imprinting and filling. You can also experiment by adding finely grated lemon zest or a ground spice to the dough to complement your choice of jam.

1¼ cups (2½ sticks) unsalted butter, softened

¾ cup granulated sugar

½ teaspoon kosher salt

2 large egg yolks

1 teaspoon pure vanilla extract

3 cups unbleached all-purpose flour

½ cup jam, jelly, preserves, or fruit spread, strained, if necessary, to remove seeds or large pieces of fruit

---

1. Preheat the oven to 350°F, with one rack in the upper third and one rack in the lower third. Line two or four baking sheets with parchment paper or silicone baking mats.

2. In the bowl of a standing mixer fitted with the paddle attachment (or with a handheld mixer), beat together the butter, sugar, and salt on medium speed until light and creamy, about 5 minutes. Mix in the egg yolks, one at a time, beating well and stopping and scraping down the bowl after each addition. Mix in the vanilla. On low speed, add the flour, about 1 cup at a time, and mix just until combined.

3. Use a melon baller, small ice cream scoop, or a measuring spoon to scoop out a rounded teaspoon of the dough, and then roll it between floured palms into a ball. Arrange the balls about 1 inch apart on the prepared baking sheets. (If you are using four baking sheets, you can form the second batch while the first batch bakes. If you are using two sheets, wait for the pans to cool after baking the first batch before forming the second batch.)

4. Using a wine cork, the rounded handle tip of a wooden spoon, or your thumb, make an indentation in the center of each ball of dough. Put the jam into a bowl and stir to loosen it. (You may wish to warm it to loosen it further.) Using a ¼-teaspoon measure, fill the indentations generously with the jam. (The jam will shrink a bit as it bakes and cools.)

5. Bake the cookies two sheets at a time until the cookie edges just begin to color, about 12 minutes, switching the pans between the racks and rotating them front to back about halfway through baking. Let the cookies cool on the pans on wire racks for 5 minutes, then, using a spatula, transfer them to the racks to cool completely.

6. Pack the cooled cookies between layers of waxed paper in an airtight container and store at room temperature for up to 1 week or in the freezer for up to 1 month.

∾ FARM JOURNAL ∾

Some of the best jams, jellies, and preserves I have tasted are the ones featuring local fruits and flavorings at farmers' markets. Rachel Saunders of Blue Chair Fruit Company in Alameda, California, brews her inspired potions in French copper pots, including strawberry-Marsala jam with rosemary and apricot jam perfumed with rose water. The equally creative and meticulous June Taylor makes bergamot marmalade and Arctic Rose white nectarine and Rose geranium conserve in nearby Berkeley. At Wilklow Orchards, in New York's Hudson Valley, "Grandma Apple" makes jams and jellies in more traditional flavors, like strawberry rhubarb and Bing cherry.

DESSERTS BETWEEN SEASONS:

DRIED FRUITS, NUTS & HERBS

If fruit is flavorful when it is picked, it will be even more so after drying has evaporated the water and concentrated its natural sugars and flavor. At farmers' markets, you will find not only the usual dried figs, prunes, and raisins, but also varieties of dried apricots, plums, Pluots, cherries, and many other dried fruits rarely seen on supermarket shelves. The long shelf life of dried fruits means that you can make desserts with vivid fruit flavors year-round, even during the months when there isn't much fresh fruit to choose from at the market.

Nuts offer another opportunity for off-season creativity. Although they often are used to embellish desserts, their flavor can also play a leading role. A member of the rose family, almonds are one of two hundred species of the genus *Prunus*, which also includes stone fruits, such as apricots, cherries, and peaches. Hazelnuts are rich and buttery with a hint of sweetness. The walnut's complexity comes, in part, from the tannins in the papery skin that covers the nut inside the shell. Toasting any of these nuts intensifies their wonderful flavors (see page 26).

Dried fruits and nuts have an affinity for each other, so I've paired them up in Not-Your-Typical Holiday Fruitcake (page 182), Cranberry-Pecan Tart in a Cocoa Crust (page 184), Fruit & Nut Chocolate Bark with Fleur de Sel (page 187), and Chocolate Prune Walnut Torte (page 198).

Herbs, like nuts, add vibrancy and flavor when not much else is available to do that job. They may be seasonal or year-round, depending on the herb and growing location. Some farmers' market vendors sell herb plants in addition to cut herbs. For your favorite herbs, purchase plants and find the right spot to grow them at home. Growing a pot of spearmint is easy and will supply you with the mint used as a flavoring or garnish throughout this book. Lavender also is hearty and prolific, and provides the flower buds needed for Lavender Walnut Sandies (page 194). Lemon verbena is used as the primary flavoring in the Lemon Verbena Buttermilk Ice Cream with Berry Sauce (page 197), and as an accent in Chilled Plum Soup with Sour Cream (page 47).

Selecting and Storing Dried Fruits, Nuts, and Herbs

If you can, taste dried fruits before purchasing to select the ones you like best. While sulfur compounds used in drying help to protect their color and keep them moist, I prefer unsulfured fruits for their clean flavor. Store dried fruits in an airtight container at room temperature to retain as much moisture as possible. If the fruit seems too dry or leathery, you can revive it by plumping it for 30 minutes in warm water, brandy, fruit juice, or another liquid compatible with the fruit and dessert. Drain off the soaking liquid before using the fruit and, if appropriate, use the liquid in the recipe.

At many farmers' markets, shoppers can find nuts both shelled and unshelled. The shell provides protection and preserves freshness, but it takes work to remove. Because nuts at the market are likely to be very fresh, you can purchase shelled ones with confidence, especially if you have sampled them. Nuts can easily turn rancid because of their high oil content. To keep them fresh longer, store them in an airtight container or zipper-top bag in the freezer. They are easier to grind finely without turning to a paste when they are frozen, too. For the best flavor, toast nuts just before you plan to use them. If toasting them directly from the freezer, allow a little extra time for them to warm before they begin to toast.

Purchase herbs that look fresh and bright and smell fragrant, passing up any that show signs of wilting. When using herbs from your own plants, pick them just before using. Refrigerate cut herbs still on the stem in a glass of water, covering the glass loosely with a plastic bag. To freeze herbs, finely chop them and pack them into ice cube trays, cover with water, and freeze. Once frozen, transfer the cubes to a zipper-top freezer bag. To use, pop out a cube and either thaw to release the herb, or if making an infusion, drop in the whole cube.

CHERRY–CHOCOLATE CHUNK COOKIES

MAKES

32

COOKIES

These cookies are the perfect dessert for Valentine's Day, when fresh fruits are scarce and markets are brimming with dried fruits. They're pretty darned compelling the rest of the year, too. The kirsch, brandy traditionally distilled from the juice of the black Morello cherry, permeates the chocolate, adding a subtle cherry flavor throughout.

SEASON TO TASTE: I prefer tart cherries for these, but if you have other varieties of locally grown dried cherries in your area, use them. Or, substitute dried cranberries. If you like your cookies with nuts, add ½ cup chopped toasted pecans or walnuts along with the chips and cherries.

1 cup unbleached all-purpose flour

½ cup unsweetened natural cocoa powder (not Dutch processed)

½ teaspoon baking powder

¼ teaspoon baking soda

½ teaspoon kosher salt

4 tablespoons (½ stick) unsalted butter, softened

½ cup granulated sugar

⅓ cup gently packed light or dark brown sugar

2 large eggs

2 teaspoons kirsch, or 1 teaspoon pure vanilla extract

1 cup (6 ounces) semisweet chocolate chips or hand-cut bittersweet chocolate chunks

¾ cup unsweetened dried cherries, coarsely chopped if large

1. Preheat the oven to 350°F, with one rack in the upper third and one rack in the lower third. Line two baking sheets with silicone baking mats or parchment paper.

2. Whisk together the flour, cocoa powder, baking powder, baking soda, and salt in a bowl. Set aside.

3. Using a handheld mixer on medium speed, beat together the butter, granulated sugar, and brown sugar until well blended. Mix in the eggs, one at a time, beating well and stopping and scraping the sides of the bowl after each addition. Stir in the kirsch, then, on low speed, mix in the flour mixture just until combined. Stir in the chocolate chips and cherries with a wooden spoon. The mixture will be thick and sticky.

4. Scoop out generous tablespoons of the dough onto the prepared baking sheets, spacing about 1 inch apart. Flatten each slightly with dampened fingers (messy but fun!) or the back of a spoon.

5. Bake just until the cookies have lost their shine, 8 to 10 minutes, switching the pans between the racks and rotating the pans front to back about halfway through baking. They will be soft, but will firm to a perfect, firm-chewy consistency as they cool. Let cool in the pans on wire racks for 5 minutes, then, using a spatula, transfer them to the racks to cool completely.

6. Pack the cooled cookies between layers of waxed paper in an airtight container and store at room temperature for up to 4 days.

NOT-YOUR-TYPICAL HOLIDAY FRUITCAKE

MAKES

3

SMALL LOAVES

My friend John Birdsall's buttery, brandy-soaked, fruit-packed cake convinced me that the ubiquitous holiday gift is not just for passing along. This adaptation of his cake takes advantage of the richly flavored and textured dried fruits that keep many market vendors in business during the barren winter months. Remember to soak the fruits in the brandy the day before you plan to bake the cakes.

For a moist cake with a long shelf life, swaddle the loaves in brandy-soaked cheesecloth and brush with additional brandy for up to 3 months. When I remember to get started in late September, I am ready with exceptional gifts for the holidays. John bakes his cakes in individual (1½-cup) charlotte molds, making them the perfect size for a gift. But you can also use muffin tins with oversized cups or similar-size molds, or you can do as I do and bake the cakes in small loaf pans.

SEASON TO TASTE: Choose a mix of four or five kinds of dried fruits, preferably both light and dark, such as cherries, apricots, plums, figs, black or golden raisins, and currants. If you like your fruitcake with nuts, reduce the fruit to 4 cups and add 3 cups coarsely chopped walnuts or pecans along with the fruit.

BRANDIED FRUIT

1 cup brandy, bourbon, or light rum

½ cup mild to moderately assertive honey, such as orange blossom or wildflower

1 teaspoon ground cinnamon

½ teaspoon ground allspice

¼ teaspoon ground cardamom

5 cups mixed dried fruits, cut into ¼-inch dice

¼ cup chopped Candied Citrus Peels (page 128), or finely grated zest of 1 orange and 1 lemon

¼ cup chopped crystallized ginger

1. To prepare the brandied fruit, stir together the brandy, honey, cinnamon, allspice, and cardamom in a large nonreactive bowl until the honey dissolves. Stir in the dried fruits, candied peels, and ginger. Leave to soak at room temperature for 12 to 24 hours. Pour through a strainer placed over a bowl, and let drain for 30 minutes. Transfer the fruits to a bowl and reserve the fruits and soaking liquid separately.

2. Preheat the oven to 275°F, with a rack in the lower third. Generously butter three 7½-by-3¾-by-2¼-inch loaf pans (or a similar size). Dust with flour, tapping out the excess.

3. To make the cakes, in a bowl of a standing mixer fitted with the paddle attachment (or with a handheld mixer), beat together the butter and brown sugar on medium speed until light and creamy, about 5 minutes. Mix in the eggs, one at a time, beating well and stopping and scraping down the bowl after each addition. On low speed, add the reserved soaking liquid.

CAKES

1 cup (2 sticks) unsalted butter, softened

1½ cups gently packed light brown sugar

5 large eggs

1¾ cups unbleached all-purpose flour

¾ teaspoon baking powder

½ teaspoon kosher salt

Brandy, bourbon, or light rum, for wrapping cakes

4. Sprinkle ¼ cup of the flour over the drained fruits and toss to coat evenly. Add the remaining 1½ cups flour, the baking powder, and salt to the batter and beat on low speed just until combined. Using a spatula, fold in the fruit.

5. Divide the batter evenly among the prepared pans and spread the tops. Set the pans on a rimmed baking sheet and bake until the loaves are golden at the edges and are starting to pull away from the sides of the pans, about 1½ hours, rotating the sheet front to back about halfway through baking. (Cakes baked in muffin tins or small pans will bake more quickly.) Let the cakes cool in the pans on wire racks for 10 to 15 minutes.

6. Run a thin knife around the inside edge of each pan to loosen the cake sides. Using oven mitts if needed, invert the pans onto the racks to release the cakes, then lift off the pans. Turn the cakes right-side up on the racks and let cool completely, about 2 hours.

7. To wrap the cakes, pour ⅓ cup brandy into a small bowl. Cut a piece of cheesecloth large enough to double wrap one cake, saturate the cloth in the brandy, and then wring out most of the brandy back into the bowl, leaving the cheesecloth lightly moistened. Wrap the cake snugly in the cheesecloth, then overwrap the cake in aluminum foil. Repeat with the remaining cakes. Store the wrapped cakes in a metal tin or airtight container at room temperature.

8. If aging the cakes for longer than a month, remove the foil once a month and brush the cheesecloth lightly all over with brandy, using a tablespoon or two per loaf. Rewrap the cakes in foil and return them to the tin.

9. To prevent crumbling when serving, cut the loaves in thin slices with a serrated knife, using a sawing motion.

CRANBERRY-PECAN TART IN A COCOA CRUST

MAKES

12

SERVINGS

Fresh and dried cranberries with pecans and hints of orange and maple make a festive, beautiful tart that is perfect for winter holiday celebrations. If rolling out pastry puts you off, this recipe is for you: the cocoa crust is pressed into the pan. A layer of chocolate chips between the crust and the filling is more good news for die-hard chocoholics.

SEASON TO TASTE: Substitute walnuts for the pecans. Substitute other dried fruits, such as cherries or chopped apricots, for the dried cranberries.

CRUST

½ cup (1 stick) unsalted butter, softened

⅓ cup granulated sugar

¼ cup unsweetened natural cocoa powder (not Dutch processed)

½ teaspoon pure vanilla extract

¼ teaspoon kosher salt

1 cup plus 2 tablespoons unbleached all-purpose flour

1 large egg white

½ cup coarsely chopped chocolate or semisweet chocolate chips

FILLING

3 cups fresh cranberries

4 tablespoons (½ stick) unsalted butter, cut into 4 or 5 pieces

½ cup granulated sugar

⅓ cup gently packed light brown sugar

¼ cup pure maple syrup

1. To make the crust, put the butter, sugar, cocoa powder, vanilla, and salt in a food processor and process until smooth. Add the flour and pulse until well mixed. Scrape down the bowl, then add the egg white and process until the dough rides on the blade in a ball.

2. Press the dough in an even layer first onto the sides and then over the bottom of an 11-by-1-inch (or 9-by-1½-inch) tart pan with a removable bottom. Preheat the oven to 325°F, with a rack in the center and a rimless baking sheet centered on the rack. Put the crust into the freezer while the oven heats, at least 10 minutes.

3. Prick the chilled crust all over with a fork, then set the tart pan on the preheated baking sheet and bake until the crust is firm, about 20 minutes. Transfer the tart pan to a wire rack and sprinkle the chocolate evenly over the warm crust. Wait 1 minute, then spread the chocolate evenly over the bottom of the crust. Raise the oven temperature to 375°F.

4. To make the filling, stir together 2 cups of the fresh cranberries, the butter, granulated sugar, brown sugar, maple syrup, orange liqueur (if using), orange zest, and salt in a heavy nonreactive saucepan over medium heat. Bring to a rolling boil and boil without stirring until most of the cranberries have popped, about 3 minutes. (Take care, as the cranberries can be lively!)

5. Remove the pan from the heat and stir in the pecans, dried cranberries, the remaining 1 cup fresh cranberries, and the cream. Spoon and spread the cranberry filling into the chocolate-lined tart crust, smoothing the surface with an offset spatula.

2 tablespoons orange liqueur, such as Grand Marnier or Cointreau (optional)

Finely grated zest of 1 orange

½ teaspoon kosher salt

1¼ cups pecans, toasted and coarsely chopped

1 cup dried cranberries

¼ cup heavy cream

6. Set the tart pan on the baking sheet in the oven and bake until the tart is bubbling all over, about 30 minutes. Let cool completely in the pan on a wire rack, about 1½ hours.

7. Center the cooled tart on a glass or small bowl to allow the outer ring to fall away. Transfer the tart, still on the pan base, to a serving plate. (Alternatively, use a large metal spatula or small rimless baking sheet to slide the tart from its base onto the plate.) Cut the tart with a thin, long, sharp knife, dipping the blade into hot water and wiping it clean with a damp kitchen towel between slices.

8. Store leftover tart, tightly covered, at room temperature for up to 3 days.

FRUIT & NUT CHOCOLATE BARK WITH FLEUR DE SEL

MAKES
36
PIECES

This candy is a great way to use nuts and dried fruits from the market during the months when fresh fruit is in short supply. It is perfect for holiday gifts or for keeping on hand for guests.

Melting part of the chocolate and then slowly stirring in the rest is an easy way to temper it, assuring the best texture and a dark, shiny surface. Don't be put off if your tempering doesn't work perfectly: the white spots or streaks that may develop on the surface are harmless and the bark will still be delicious. The drizzled white chocolate is not as fussy, and you can save time by melting it in a microwave, rather than washing and reusing the double boiler. Be sure to use a good-quality white chocolate, one made with cocoa butter and no added vegetable oils.

The salt should be medium-fine and a little briny for an occasional flavor "pop" that nicely balances the sweet fruit and toasted nuts.

SEASON TO TASTE: Use other types of toasted nuts or dried fruits, one type of each or in combination. Walnuts, blanched hazelnuts, dried apricots or mangoes, or unsweetened dried blueberries are good choices. (Cut any large pieces of fruit into pieces about the size of a raisin.) A topping of chopped crystallized ginger or unsweetened shredded dried coconut are other pleasing additions.

12 ounces bittersweet chocolate (60 to 70 percent cacao), cut into roughly ½-inch pieces

¾ cup pecans, pistachios, or blanched almonds, toasted and coarsely chopped

¼ teaspoon sea salt, such as fleur de sel or gray salt

¾ cup dried cranberries or unsweetened dried cherries, cut into raisin size if large

2 ounces white chocolate, chopped

1. Line a rimless baking sheet at least 10 inches square with aluminum foil.

2. Set aside about one-third (about 4 ounces) of the bittersweet chocolate, selecting the largest pieces. Melt the remaining two-thirds in the top of a double boiler over (but not touching) gently simmering water, stirring with a wooden spoon or silicone spatula until it is completely melted and perfectly smooth and registers 115° to 120°F on an instant-read thermometer.

3. Remove the top of the double boiler from the heat and stir the chocolate until it registers 95° to 100°F. Add the reserved chocolate pieces and stir continuously until smooth. Remove any solid pieces and reserve for another use.

CONTINUED >

4. Without delay, stir in the nuts, then pour the chocolate onto the foil-lined baking sheet and spread it with an offset spatula to cover a 9- to 10-inch square. (It does not need to be perfectly square.) Sprinkle lightly with the salt, and scatter the dried fruit evenly over the surface while the chocolate is still soft.

5. Put the white chocolate in a microwave-safe bowl and heat at 50 percent power for 1 minute, then give it a stir. If it is not fully melted, microwave longer, checking every 20 to 30 seconds, until you can stir the chocolate smooth. Dip a fork or whisk in the melted white chocolate and wave it over the dark chocolate square, drizzling an attractive pattern on top.

6. Refrigerate or freeze the chocolate slab on the baking sheet just until it is set and no longer shiny, about 15 minutes. Transfer the foil to a flat surface and, using a sharp, heavy knife, cut the bark into six equal strips in one direction, and then six equal strips in the other direction. (Alternatively, cut or break the bark into uneven pieces.) Carefully peel the bark pieces from the foil.

7. Store the bark, separating the layers with waxed paper, in an airtight container in a cool, dry place for up to 2 weeks.

HAZELNUT-ALMOND BISCOTTI

The term *biscotti* is formed from two Italian words: *bis*, or "twice," and *cotto*, or "baked." The cookies are baked in long logs, then cut and baked a second time for a crunchy biscuit that is ideal for soaking up coffee, tea, milk, or vin santo. These are tender enough to enjoy without dunking, on their own or as an embellishment to creamy desserts like Tangerine-sicle Ice Cream (page 111) and Roasted Peach Melba (page 35). Nut oil supercharges their nutty flavor.

SEASON TO TASTE: You can substitute your favorite nuts for the hazelnuts and almonds and use other nut oils, or even a mild olive oil. La Tourangelle makes exceptional nut oils, including almond, walnut, hazelnut, pecan, and pistachio, among others (see Sources & Resources, page 200).

1½ cups unbleached all-purpose flour

1 teaspoon baking powder

½ teaspoon baking soda

½ teaspoon kosher salt

½ cup granulated sugar

¼ cup hazelnut, almond, or walnut oil

2 large eggs

½ teaspoon pure vanilla extract

½ teaspoon finely grated orange or lemon zest

½ cup hazelnuts, toasted, peels rubbed off, and coarsely chopped

½ cup blanched or natural almonds, toasted

1. Preheat the oven to 325°F, with a rack near the center. Line a baking sheet with a silicone baking mat or parchment paper.

2. Stir together the flour, baking powder, baking soda, and salt in a small bowl. Set aside.

3. Whisk together the sugar, oil, eggs, vanilla, and orange zest in a bowl until well combined. Stir in the flour mixture with a wooden spoon to form a dough. Mix in the nuts.

4. Divide the dough in half. Shape each half into a log about 10 inches long and 2 inches wide on the prepared baking sheet, allowing at least 1 inch on all sides of each log to allow for spreading. Bake until firm to the touch and light brown, about 30 minutes. Transfer the logs with the mat or parchment to a wire rack to cool for 15 to 20 minutes. Reduce the oven temperature to 275°F.

5. Transfer the partially cooled logs to a cutting board. Using a serrated knife and cutting with a sawing motion, trim off the ends at a slight angle (baker's snack!), and cut the logs into ⅜- to ½-inch-thick slices.

CONTINUED >

6. Return the mat or parchment to the baking sheet and place the biscotti, cut-side down, on the sheet. (They can be close together.) Bake until golden, about 35 minutes. Let cool completely in the pan on a wire rack.

7. Store the biscotti in an airtight container at room temperature for up to 3 weeks, or freeze in a zipper-top freezer bag for up to 2 months.

∾ FARM JOURNAL ∾

According to the Hazelnut Council, there are more than one hundred varieties of hazelnuts grown throughout the world, with the majority grown in Turkey. In North America, the Willamette Valley of Oregon boasts the largest production, with smaller crops grown in Washington, California, and British Columbia.

LAVENDER WALNUT SANDIES

MAKES

5

DOZEN COOKIES

These cookies are rich and buttery, with an alluring sandy texture and a delicate lavender essence. Use the freshest, highest-quality butter you can put your hands on. If you have a butter vendor at your market, that's the butter to buy.

Pick the lavender blossoms from their stems and leave them to dry for at least 3 days before grinding them, or purchase dried lavender buds meant for culinary use. The cookies can be made in advance up to the final slicing and baking: wrap the dough tightly in plastic film and refrigerate for up to 1 week, or overwrap with aluminum foil and freeze for up to 1 month. No need to thaw—just slice and bake.

SEASON TO TASTE: Experiment with herbs that have a sweet bent, such as lemon thyme, lemon balm, or pineapple sage, in place of the lavender. And try pecans in place of the walnuts.

3 teaspoons dried lavender blossoms

2 tablespoons turbinado, Demerara, or other coarse sugar

½ cup granulated sugar

1 cup (2 sticks) unsalted butter, softened

½ teaspoon kosher salt

2 cups unbleached all-purpose flour

1 cup walnuts, toasted and chopped medium-fine

1. Put 1 teaspoon of the lavender blossoms in a spice grinder and pulse until they are in very small pieces. Stir together the ground lavender and turbinado sugar in a small bowl. Set aside for coating the cookie log.

2. Put the granulated sugar and the remaining 2 teaspoons lavender blossoms in a food processor and process until the sugar is the texture of confectioners' sugar. Add the butter and salt and process until smooth and creamy, about 1 minute, stopping to scrape down the bowl as needed. Add the flour and walnuts and pulse several times until the dough is well blended and begins to ride on the blade in a ball.

3. Transfer the dough to a lightly floured work surface and gather into a mass. Divide the dough in half, and shape each half into a log about 8 inches long and 1½ inches in diameter.

4. Lay two sheets of plastic film, each about 12 inches long, on a flat surface. Spread half of the reserved lavender sugar down the center of each piece, shaping it into a strip about 3 inches wide and 8 inches long.

5. Lay one dough log on the edge of a lavender-sugar strip and roll it across the sugar to coat evenly. Wrap the log tightly in the plastic film. Repeat with the second log and the second lavender-sugar strip. Refrigerate the wrapped logs until firm, at least 2 hours.

6. Preheat the oven to 350°F, with one rack in the upper third and one rack in the lower third. Line two baking sheets with silicone baking mats or parchment paper.

7. Unwrap one log. Using a sharp, heavy knife, cut the log into ¼-inch-thick slices. (If the slices crumble, try cutting them a little thicker.) Evenly space the cookies on one of the prepared baking sheets, about 1 inch apart. Repeat with the other log.

8. Bake until the cookies begin to color at the edges, 13 to 15 minutes, switching the pans between the racks and rotating them front to back about halfway through baking. Transfer the cookies on the parchment or silicone mats to wire racks to cool completely.

9. Pack the cooled cookies between layers of waxed paper in an airtight container and store at room temperature for up to 2 weeks.

LEMON VERBENA BUTTERMILK ICE CREAM WITH BERRY SAUCE

MAKES ABOUT

8

**SERVINGS,
OR 1 QUART**

This refreshing citrus-herbal ice cream is made tangy with buttermilk and crème fraîche. It is also delicious with the raspberry sauce used in Roasted Peach Melba (page 35) or with the rhubarb sauce used in Rhubarb, Blueberry & Cream Parfait (page 147) in place of the berry sauce. Crisp cookies round out the dish.

See Hints for Making Great Ice Cream on page 112.

SEASON TO TASTE: Substitute lemon thyme or lemon balm for the lemon verbena. Alternatively, use a 3-by-1-inch strip of lemon zest.

ICE CREAM

1 cup heavy cream or half-and-half

⅔ cup granulated sugar

¼ cup mild-flavored honey, such as acacia, alfalfa, or clover

¼ teaspoon kosher salt

⅓ cup firmly packed fresh lemon verbena leaves

1 cup buttermilk

1 cup crème fraîche

⅓ cup fresh lemon juice (2 to 3 lemons)

SAUCE

½ pint (about 1 cup) blackberries

½ pint (about 1 cup) blueberries

½ pint (about 1 cup) raspberries

¼ cup granulated sugar

Juice of ½ lemon

1. To make the ice cream, stir together the cream, sugar, honey, and salt in a small nonreactive saucepan over medium heat until steam rises from the surface and bubbles begin to form along the edge of the pan. Remove from the heat and stir in the lemon verbena. Set aside to steep for 20 minutes.

2. Pour the mixture through a fine-mesh strainer placed over a bowl, pressing on the leaves to extract as much flavor as possible. Whisk in the buttermilk, crème fraîche, and lemon juice. Cover and refrigerate until very cold, several hours, or place in the freezer for about 1 hour.

3. Freeze the ice-cream base in an ice-cream maker according to the manufacturer's instructions. Transfer to an airtight container and press a piece of plastic film or waxed paper directly on the surface of the ice cream before covering. Freeze until the desired consistency, about 2 hours or up to 1 week.

4. To make the sauce, gently stir together all the berries and the sugar in a nonreactive saucepan over medium-low heat until the sugar is completely dissolved and the mixture is very juicy, about 2 minutes. Remove from the heat and stir in the lemon juice. Let cool to room temperature, then refrigerate, covered, until serving time or up to 3 days.

5. Scoop the ice cream into bowls and top with some of the berry sauce.

CHOCOLATE PRUNE WALNUT TORTE

With this rich torte on hand, I never feel deprived during the eight-day Passover holiday, when Jews abstain from eating leavened grains. Here, ground nuts and egg whites take the place of flour and leavening. Prunes intensify the chocolate's fruity flavors and keep the torte moist and chewy. The torte can be prepared by hand, but a food processor and standing mixer make it easy as pie.

SEASON TO TASTE: Substitute almonds, pecans, or hazelnuts for all or part of the walnuts. Omit the berries when they are not in season.

TORTE

9 ounces bittersweet chocolate (60 to 70 percent cacao), coarsely chopped

1½ cups walnut pieces, toasted and coarsely chopped

1¼ cups (about 7 ounces) pitted prunes

6 large egg whites, at room temperature

¼ teaspoon kosher salt

½ cup granulated sugar

¼ teaspoon pure vanilla extract, or seeds scraped from 1 vanilla bean, split lengthwise

1 cup heavy cream, very cold

1 tablespoon plus 2 teaspoons granulated sugar

1 pint (2 cups) raspberries or blackberries

1. Preheat the oven to 325°F, with a rack near the center. Line the bottom of a 9-by-3-inch springform pan with parchment paper. Oil the sides of the pan but not the pan bottom or the parchment.

2. To make the torte, pulse the chocolate in a food processor until it is in small pieces. Add the nuts and continue pulsing until finely chopped. Add the prunes and pulse a few more times until the mixture looks like moist cookie crumbs. Set aside.

3. In the bowl of a standing mixer fitted with the whisk attachment (or with a handheld mixer), beat together the egg whites and salt on medium speed until they hold soft peaks. Increase the speed to medium-high and add the sugar, 1 tablespoon at a time, beating for about 30 seconds after each addition. When all of the sugar has been added, continue to beat for a few minutes longer until the whites are smooth and glossy and hold firm peaks. Add the vanilla and beat just until mixed.

4. Use your hands to break up and sprinkle a large handful of the chocolate mixture over the egg whites, then use a spatula to fold it into the whites just until combined. Continue sprinkling and folding until you have added all of the chocolate mixture. As you fold, be sure to scrape along the bottom of the bowl. Don't worry if the whites deflate a bit.

5. Without delay, turn the mixture into the prepared pan and smooth the top. Bake until the torte no longer feels jiggly when you lightly press it with your fingertip near the center, about 45 minutes,

rotating the pan front to back about halfway through the baking time. Let the torte cool completely in the pan on a wire rack, about 1 hour.

6. To unmold, run a thin knife around the inside edge of the pan to loosen the torte sides. Unclasp and lift the outside ring from the springform pan. Invert a flat plate over the torte and then quickly invert the plate and pan bottom. Remove the pan bottom and peel off the parchment, then invert the torte again onto a serving plate. It may fall slightly in the center as it cools, making a perfect hollow to fill with the cream and berries.

7. Using a chilled bowl and a chilled whisk or beaters, whip the cream with the 2 teaspoons sugar to medium peaks. Cover and refrigerate until serving. About 15 minutes before serving, gently stir together the remaining 1 tablespoon sugar and the berries in a bowl and set aside.

8. Just before serving, pile the cream onto the center of the cake and sprinkle with the berries, drizzling any juices from the bottom of the bowl over them. Cut the torte with a thin, long, sharp knife, dipping the blade into hot water and wiping it clean with a damp kitchen towel between slices.

9. Store leftover torte, tightly covered, in the refrigerator for up to 3 days.

∾ FARM JOURNAL ∾

The folks responsible for marketing prunes think "dried plums" sounds more appealing. Of course, that's all prunes are, but the ones typically known as prunes are made from the meaty, elongated plum varieties that are called prune plums, even when they are sold fresh. Try the torte with any dried plums you find at your farmers' market.

SOURCES & RESOURCES

Many Web sites list farmers' markets. Put "farmers market" and your county, city, or town into an Internet search engine and see what comes up. You may also find a state or regional farmers' market association that will direct you to markets in your area. The following directories can help you locate farmers' markets where you live or where you may be traveling.

FARMERS' MARKETS

Kaiser Permanente farmers' markets:
www.members.kaiserpermanente.org/redirects/farmersmarkets/
Local Harvest: www.localharvest.org/farmers-markets
Rodale Institute's Farm Locator:
www.rodaleinstitute.org/farm_locator
United States Department of Agriculture (USDA):
www.apps.ams.usda.gov/FarmersMarkets/

FARMING AND SUSTAINABLE AGRICULTURE

The Center for Urban Education about Sustainable Agriculture: www.cuesa.org
Community Alliance with Family Farmers: www.caff.org
Council on the Environment of New York City, Greenmarkets: www.cenyc.org/greenmarket
Networking Association for Farm Direct Marketing and Agritourism (NAFDMA): www.nafdma.com
Stone Barns Center for Food & Agriculture:
www.stonebarnscenter.org

FARMS AND PRODUCERS MENTIONED IN *FARMERS' MARKET DESSERTS*

Blue Chair Fruit Company: www.bluechairfruit.com
C. J. Olson Cherries: www.cjolsoncherries.com
Claude Richmond Maple Syrup (no Web site)
Cypress Grove Chêvre: www.cypressgrovechevre.com

Dateland: www.dateland.com
Frog Hollow Farm: www.froghollow.com
Glaum Egg Ranch: www.glaumeggranch.com
Hamada Farms:
www.cuesa.org/markets/farmers/farm_39.php
Jensen Orchard (no Web site)
June Taylor Company: www.junetaylorjams.com
Marshall's Farm Natural Honey: www.marshallshoney.com
Mead Orchard: www.meadorchards.com
Potter Cranberry Company (no Web site)
Redwood Hill Farm: www.redwoodhill.com
Ronnybrook Farm Dairy: www.ronnybrook.com
Swanton Berry Farms: www.swantonberryfarm.com
Tairwá-Knoll Farms: www.knollorganics.com
Warwick Valley Winery & Distillery: www.wvwinery.com
Weston's Antique Apples: www.westonapples.com
Wild Hive Farm: www.wildhivefarm.com
Wilklow Orchards: www.wilkloworchards.com
Windrose Farm: www.windrosefarm.org

BAKING AND DESSERT TECHNIQUES

The number of Web sites and blogs with recipes and cooking information seems to grow exponentially each day. The following are a few I visit for inspiration or information on baking techniques and ingredients. Many of the market, producer, ingredient, and equipment sites listed here also contain useful information.

www.101cookbooks.com
www.baking911.com
www.betterbaking.com
www.chezpim.typepad.com/blogs
www.chocolateandzucchini.com
www.davidlebovitz.com
www.eggbeater.typepad.com
www.exploratorium.edu/cooking
www.joyofbaking.com

INGREDIENTS AND EQUIPMENT

Look to the following sources for items you are unable to find in your area. Many of them also provide extensive information on their products or on baking.

A.G. FERRARI
www.agferrari.com
Wide variety of Italian ingredients.

BOB'S RED MILL NATURAL FOODS
www.bobsredmill.com
Wide selection of flours, grains, sugars, spices, and other products.

BRIDGE KITCHENWARE
www.bridgekitchenware.com
Extensive collection of cooking, baking, and pastry equipment, from accessories to appliances.

BROADWAY PANHANDLER
www.broadwaypanhandler.com
Bakeware, cookware, kitchen tools, and tabletop supplies.

CHOCOSPHERE
www.chocosphere.com
Chocolate and related products from around the world, including many organic brands.

DIVINE CHOCOLATE
www.divinechocolateusa.com
A farmer-owned fair trade company producing excellent chocolate.

GUSTIAMO
www.gustiamo.com
Italian ingredients.

KING ARTHUR FLOUR
www.kingarthurflour.com
Information about baking, as well as flour and other baking ingredients and equipment.

LA TOURANGELLE
www.latourangelle.com
Artisanal nut, seed, and other oils.

MONIN
www.monin.com
Flavoring syrups.

NATIONAL HONEY BOARD
www.honeylocator.com/index.asp
Information about honey, descriptions of honey varieties, and a "honey locator" to help you find varieties available in your state.

PENZEYS SPICES
www.penzeys.com
Quality herbs, spices, extracts, and seasonings.

PUSH BUTTON CHERRY PITTER
www.pushbuttoncherrypitter.com

THE SPANISH TABLE
www.spanishtable.com
Spanish and Portuguese ingredients, including wines, available online and at stores in Seattle, Berkeley, and Santa Fe.

SUR LA TABLE
www.surlatable.com
Bakeware, cookware, and kitchen accessories available in retail stores, by mail-order catalog, and online.

TORANI
www.torani.com
Flavoring syrups.

THE VANILLA COMPANY
www.vanilla.com
Vanilla facts, lore, and tips, as well as sustainably produced vanilla products.

WILLIAMS-SONOMA
www.williams-sonoma.com
Bakeware, wineglasses, and other kitchen and tableware available in retail stores, by mail-order catalog, and online.

ZINGERMAN'S
www.zingermans.com
Specialty grocery.

INDEX

TABLE OF EQUIVALENTS

The exact equivalents in the following tables have been rounded for convenience.

LIQUID/DRY MEASURES

U.S.	Metric
¼ teaspoon	1.25 milliliters
½ teaspoon	2.5 milliliters
1 teaspoon	5 milliliters
1 tablespoon (3 teaspoons)	15 milliliters
1 fluid ounce (2 tablespoons)	30 milliliters
¼ cup	60 milliliters
⅓ cup	80 milliliters
½ cup	120 milliliters
1 cup	240 milliliters
1 pint (2 cups)	480 milliliters
1 quart (4 cups, 32 ounces)	960 milliliters
1 gallon (4 quarts)	3.84 liters
1 ounce (by weight)	28 grams
1 pound	454 grams
2.2 pounds	1 kilogram

LENGTH

U.S.	Metric
⅛ inch	3 millimeters
¼ inch	6 millimeters
½ inch	12 millimeters
1 inch	2.5 centimeters

OVEN TEMPERATURE

Fahrenheit	Celsius	Gas
250	120	½
275	140	1
300	150	2
325	160	3
350	180	4
375	190	5
400	200	6
425	220	7
450	230	8
475	240	9
500	260	10